Just Married

Margaret Feinberg

HARVEST HOUSE PUBLISHERS

EUGENE, OREGON

Cover by Terry Dugan Design, Minneapolis, Minnesota

Cover photo © Peter Correz/Stone/Getty Images

While the stories herein are all true, names have been changed to provide these couples
some privacy.

JUST MARRIED
Copyright © 2005 by Margaret Feinberg
Published by Harvest House Publishers
Eugene, Oregon 97402
www.harvesthousepublishers.com

Library of Congress Cataloging-in-Publication Data

Feinberg, Margaret, 1974–
   Just married / Margaret Feinberg.
        p. cm.
   ISBN 0-7369-1507-9 (pbk.)
   1. Spouses—Religious life.   2. Young adults—Religious life.   3. Marriage—Religious aspects—
Christianity. I. Title.
   BV4529.2.F44 2005
   248.8'44—dc22   2004024317

Printed in the United States of America

   05   06   07   08   09   10   11   12 / VP-MS /   10   9   8   7   6   5   4   3   2   1

Dedicated to

*William and Marjane Feinberg and Gary and Coke Oines,
who have demonstrated the wonder of marriage
for more than seven decades.*

Acknowledgments

Thanks to Brent and Karen Cunningham, who graciously opened up their home for young couples to meet for more than a year. I'm grateful for Natalie Gillespie for her friendship and contributions to this book—which were invaluable. Thank you to Leif, who wrote the chapter titled "For Him Only" and allowed me to take our relationship public. And thank you to the entire Harvest House team—Barb Sherrill, Carolyn McCready, Brynn Thomas, Kim Moore, and, of course, Terry Glaspey, who continues to make us laugh out loud.

Contents

The Wonder Years

TO BE A NEWLYWED IS TO BE FULL OF WONDER. It's an incredible time of celebration, excitement, and joy all rolled into one. For many, it's the fulfillment of lifelong dreams and prayers. It's new. It's fresh. It's also very real. Getting married is a time of transition, growth, and the blending of two lives that, at times, couldn't seem more different.

I'm not quite sure when you officially stop being a newlywed. I don't think anyone has determined the exact date. Do you stop being a newlywed after three months of marriage, six months, or a year? I have talked to people who have been married for three, five, and even 30 years, and they say they still feel like newlyweds. If I catch them at just the right time, they look like it too. A loving glance. A squeeze of the knee. A tender kiss.

I don't know when the newlywed stage ends, but I hope it doesn't happen to me. If it does, I want to get it back again (with the same partner). Maybe you feel that way too. Sure, I want to know more about my spouse, continue to grow in familiarity, and share life experiences, and one day I really do want to win the debates over which way the toilet paper should be hung on the roll and whether to squeeze the tube of toothpaste from the top, bottom, or middle. In the meantime, I never want to grow so accustomed to this wonderful gift God has entrusted me with that I grow complacent, cold-hearted, or unforgiving.

I've watched people observe my husband and me sitting shoulder to shoulder in a meeting or movie and comment, "They're newlyweds." One woman who watched us fawn over each other actually rolled her eyes and said, "Oh, that will end one day."

I bristle at the thought—because I've found love, and more than anything I want to keep that love alive. I know it's not going to be easy. The statistics tell us that much. Wisdom tells me that eventually the energy, excitement, and vitality of these early days will fade, but still I don't believe that passion has to have an expiration date. Just look at the couples in their eighties still holding hands.

The true beauty of marriage will never be found in the latest sex article in *Cosmo* or that big lacy box of waxy chocolates on

---

Tying the Knot

- Nearly 6400 people get married every day.

- Approximately 2.3 million marriages take place in the United States annually.

- Nevada is the most popular state for marriages. Seventy-five marriages are performed in Nevada per every 1000 residents annually, many of which take place in Las Vegas. Hawaii ranks second, with 20 marriages per 1000 residents, and Arkansas third, with 15 marriages per 1000 residents.

- The estimated U.S. median age at first marriage for women is 25.1.

- The estimated U.S. median age at first marriage for men is 26.8.*

FOOTNOTE

* (Taken from: www.cdc.gov/nchs/, www.cdc.gov/nchs/datawh/statab/unpubd/nvstab50.htm, and www.census.gov/Press-Release/www/2001/cb01-113.html)

Valentine's Day. Those are cheap substitutes for what real marriage is about: the day-to-day, humble act of two people committed to live life together no matter what tomorrow may bring. Maybe, just maybe, with enough prayer, determination, and humor, we can learn to keep the wonder and appreciation of being *Just Married* forever.

—Margaret Feinberg

Some Things Never Change

one

*Take each other for
better or worse, but
not for granted.*

—Arlene Dahl

My husband and I just got back from a romantic whisk-away weekend to an island cabin on a nearby shore.

Well, technically, it wasn't very "whisk-away," since we had to plan it two months in advance because our lives and schedules are insanely busy. And I guess you can't really call it a "weekend," since my husband got called into work at the last minute and we were only able to spend one night at the cabin. And maybe "romantic" is a stretch too, since we ate a candle-less taco dinner on paper plates.

But it was our first attempt at a romantic whisk-away weekend. We're new at this sort of thing, and we're determined to get better at it. Next time we'll pack the candles, steak, salad, and thinly sliced potatoes. We'll bring a cooler with chilled cheesecake and sparkling cider. We'll bring eggs, fresh fruit, baked goods, and French vanilla coffee for breakfast. We'll pack romantic CDs and DVDs, games that will make us laugh, and soft blankets that will keep us warm. And in the end, we'll have enough bags to make people think we're going to be gone for an entire month.

Not too long ago, I entered the world of being a newlywed, and I'm still trying to play catch-up. Whether it's learning how to plan for a romantic whisk-away weekend, merge two checking accounts, or avoid arguing over the dumbest little things, I've discovered I have a lot to discover. But even with the steep learning curve, I am grateful to be married. Now, don't get me wrong. I thoroughly enjoyed my seemingly carefree days of being single, when I could jet off to see friends for the weekend (assuming I could live with the aftermath of credit card debt), drink milk out of the carton without feeling guilty or like a hypocrite, leave dirty dishes sitting for days on end without being held accountable, and shop without anyone asking, "You bought what?"

Yep. Those were the days. Now these are the days, and they are rich and textured and filled with more mystery, wonder, and reasons to laugh than I could have ever imagined. Some days marriage feels like a long catnap, nestled next to a window where the sun's rays warm my soul. Other days marriage feels like a tender embrace that whispers, "You're not alone anymore." And then there are the days marriage feels like a display window as the innermost parts of my soul take center stage when I deal with fears, insecurities, and doubts.

At times marriage still feels like a strange phenomenon. I am no longer daydreaming about what my spouse will be like—I can reach out and touch his fingers and count his toes. I can choose between pinching myself and pinching him, and no matter which one of us I squeeze, he is still real (though getting the yelp out of him is usually more fun). Marriage has awakened my entire being to new experiences, encounters, and viewpoints. It has enlarged me as an individual.

Quick Tip: Turn off the television.

However, for all the good that has been worked in and through me so far, don't think for a moment that this mysterious holy union is simple or can be done well while catnapping—especially during those first few years when two people have to agree to make a small miracle happen: learn to live life together.

It doesn't matter whether your courtship was a month, a year, or a decade. Somewhere during those first few years of marriage you're going to be hit square between the eyes with the fact that there are things about your spouse that will never change. You can hope they change. You can pray they change. You can beg God to change them. Yet some things about your spouse were never meant to change. They were meant to be that way from the beginning, and they're going to be that way until the very end. I've managed to sort through a lot of never-gonna-change attributes about my spouse. Can you relate to any of them?

Never Gonna Change No. 1: My spouse has morning breath. The only thing worse than the fact that my spouse has morning breath is that I have it too. And boy, is it bad! The crazy thing is that my husband is okay with his morning breath, and the even crazier thing is that he's okay with mine too. I don't understand it. Some days—especially if I've eaten a sugary treat the night before—I wake up with this taste of roadkill in my mouth. As I snuggle into my husband's arms, I discover he was munching on the same dead animal while we were sleeping. Leif could lie there all morning quite content. As for me, I'm making a beeline for my faithful Triple-Action, Tartar-Fighting, Extra-Whitening, Ban-Bad-Breath-Forever toothpaste.

Fortunately, I have a husband who loves me and gracefully embraces my hygiene neuroses and follows me to the bathroom. Afterward we nestle back in bed with a minty fresh cloud. As long as we are alive, I don't think the whole morning breath issue will ever resolve itself beyond a bottle of Listerine. It may change a little when we get dentures and have to switch to Polident, but morning breath is something I'm never going to change about my husband or myself.

Never Gonna Change No. 2: My spouse is different from me. I never wanted to marry myself. I am not that narcissistic, but there have been more than a handful of times when I've thought to myself, *If only he were a little bit more like me, this would be a whole lot easier.* Instead, he is a whole lot like him. Imagine that! And I actually love him for it—whenever I'm not trying to convince him to change.

Never Gonna Change No. 3: My husband is a man. I'm grateful that my husband is male; don't get me wrong. I never wanted to marry a woman or someone who had played switcharoo, but as a man, Leif likes manly things like video games, paintball, and those sweaty male-bonding activities that usually involve footballs, grunting noises, and ritualistic pats on the butt. Shopping and scrapbooking will never be high on his priority list, but that is what girlfriends are for!

Never Gonna Change No. 4: My husband snores. Surprises are part of married life. They just come with the territory. One of those little surprises—the fact that my husband snores—has proved to be a big issue in our marriage. I don't know how this little snoring detail escaped me during the year we got to know each other before we were married, but the week after we were married, we stayed in a townhouse in Colorado. For whatever reason—attribute it to dry weather or postmarital bliss—Leif didn't snore. The first night we arrived in our new homestead in Alaska, the snoring began and hasn't stopped since.

We have tried just about everything. Maybe you have too. We tried having him sleep on his side or stomach, where he is less likely

Options for Eliminating Snoring

- Breathe Right nasal strips
- Nasal sprays
- Earplugs
- Tennis ball T-shirt
- Lose weight
- Add a fan or other white noise to drown out the sound
- Sleep testing and a CPAP machine (for sleep apnea)
- Surgery
- Last resort: sleep in separate rooms

to snore. We tried having him wear Breathe Right strips to open his nasal passages. We tried the accompanying Breathe Right saline solution that you spray up the nose (which isn't much fun). We tried sewing tennis balls in the back of a T-shirt so that every time he rolls over at night, he wakes himself up and returns to sleeping on his side. We even tried mentholated vaporizing creams.

All of these work from time to time. The problem is that none of them work consistently, and we are usually busy trying them all at the same time—never quite sure which will work.

When Leif is sick or exhausted, he steps in the ring with world-class snoring champions. And he can hold his own. I have tried wearing earplugs, which always fall out, and burying my head under multiple pillows, which tends to interfere with breathing. In the end I have discovered only one thing that works 100 percent of the time: Sleeping in the other room. That one act—sleeping apart from my spouse—is more painful than shooting saline up your taped nose while wearing tennis balls on your back and being buried under a stack of pillows. It is brutal.

I never imagined I would have to sleep apart from my spouse. In 30 years I could conceive that maybe we would have a big fight and end up in separate bedrooms for a night. I have seen that in the movies. I never thought that as blissful newlyweds my husband would be kissing me on the forehead and then going to sleep on the couch.

It has taken me a while to come to terms with the fact that the snoring issue may never go away. This is something we are going to have to live with and overcome. We have done some practical things to make it a little easier. First, Leif and I always go to bed together and spend time snuggling before we make an attempt to go to sleep snore free. Before he falls asleep, we decide on which of the "strikes" he is out. Sometimes, he only gets one or two "strikes" of snoring, where I wake him up, and then he has to head to the couch. Sometimes, he gets a "three strikes and you're out." If I wake up three times, then he has to move. Occasionally, I will fall into

Quick Tip: Be a servant.

a deep enough sleep where the snoring doesn't bother me and we'll make it through the night together. Even if we don't, we make sure he crawls back in bed with me in the morning so we can spend those precious waking up moments together. Snoring may never go away, but we're learning to work through it.

Never Gonna Change No. 5: My husband has different needs than me. I need to be loved, cared for, and nurtured. I need to be affirmed and hugged and kissed and told I'm beautiful. My husband, on the other hand, needs two things: dinner and sex. He needs love, affirmation, support, prayer, and everything else on my list, but his required portions are a lot smaller. I have to figure out how to love him in his love language rather than my own, and that's not always easy.

Never Gonna Change No. 6: My husband has annoying habits. Leif is perfect, except for one thing: He has an annoying habit. Okay, maybe two. On a bad day, three. On a terrible day, he has, well, a lot of them. On the top of the list is my husband's inability to keep track of time. He always has a dozen excuses why he doesn't wear a watch, and invariably we are either late or stressed about being late. It drives me nuts some days. I can't believe my husband's annoying habits, at least until I look at a list of my own, and then I begin to wonder, *How does he live with me?*

One of the advantages of having things about your spouse that will never change is that we are given the opportunity to influence each other's behavior in a way that is healthy and provides growth. My husband has taught me to be more laid-back, that it really is okay to eat pizza with lots of toppings every once in a while, and what it means to be observant. Meanwhile, he has learned a bit about embracing adventure. We have rubbed off on each other, and in the process we have both learned to let things go and discovered what is truly important. Together, we become more balanced individuals.

Leif has compiled his own "Never Gonna Change" list about me. Here are a few of his entries:

Never Gonna Change No. 1: My wife will always change her mind.
Whether it is about dinner, what movie she wants to watch, or what is next on our agenda, the only thing you can expect is the unexpected. Even though she says she wants something, that doesn't mean she will want it in five minutes. As a guy it makes sense to me that when she says she needs to keep from eating high-fat, high-carbohydrate foods, she means it. But every time I try to "help" her, she growls at me. Not that I am any better, of course. I manage to change my mind regarding any number of things, but my changes always make sense.

Never Gonna Change No. 2: The area around the bathroom sink is no longer mine. I knew she had a lot of stuff when we were dating, but since we were married the quantity has multiplied. I have a theory that hair products and lotions breed during the night to make as many different variations of themselves as possible. I don't know exactly what all those tubes, vials, and powders do, but I certainly like the results. I have even started letting Margaret pluck my eyebrows, though I can confidently say that the plucking stops there.

Never Gonna Change No. 3: My wife will never understand computers. I operated under a cloud of blissful ignorance regarding her lack of knowledge when it came to technical gadgets until we got married. I watched Margaret use a computer to write and assumed she knew how to use it. Little did I know that her wisdom regarding food, health, and relationships didn't translate well into keeping a computer running. Up until our first year of marriage, I had always wondered why I attended DeVry Institute of Technology. Now I think I've got it! I am supposed to use my technical knowledge so my wife doesn't lose all of her life's work by pressing the wrong button on the keyboard.

Never Gonna Change No. 4: Getting out of the shower and drying off has a different meaning for my wife. As long as she holds a towel around her for a nanosecond after stepping out of the shower, she believes she will be instantly dry. While quite attractive to look at,

Quick Tip: Eat more vegetables.

this becomes a problem when she jumps into bed and I get my second shower of the night. I know I probably need it, but I still think there would be better ways to communicate this to me.

Never Gonna Change No. 5: My wife is unable to drive down the road at a consistent speed. Instead of holding her foot steady on the gas pedal, she likes to lift it on and off at will. She slows down for fields, unusual rocks, sunsets, and just about anything else that catches her interest, which is a bit frustrating for everyone else behind her and most of all her passenger—which is usually me.

Never Gonna Change No. 6: This is just a hopeful never-gonna-change. I hope and pray my wife's love and acceptance for me will not disappear as we get older, get used to each other, and struggle against taking each other for granted. I do have bad breath pretty much all day, don't like to shower, and would rather play video games than go for a hike, but she chose to say "I do" anyway. So even though I wonder how mentally balanced she might be for vowing that, I am and eternally will be thankful to God for blessing me with such a wonderful friend, wife, and lover.

Questions for Reflection

1. What things are never going to change about your spouse? What things are never going to change about you?

2. Which things were never meant to change?

3. Which items on your spouse's "Never Gonna Change" list cause you to laugh?

4. In what ways will you learn to accept your spouse's annoying habits without building resentment? (Will you learn to pick up his socks without comment?)

5. In what ways does your marriage give you the opportunity to become more well-rounded?

12 Sure-Fire Ways to Kick Off World War III (or at Least Make Your Spouse Really, Really Upset)

one Respond to everything your spouse says for the next seven days with "That sounds nice, honey."

two When your spouse asks you to do something, say "Yes" and then go do something else.

three Refuse to do dishes, clean, pick up, put gas in the car, or pay a bill for 30 days.

four Eat beans for the next two weeks for breakfast, lunch, and dinner.

five Hide the laundry detergent.

six Go shopping and buy everything you see.

seven Throw away all of your bills.

eight Talk about yourself all the time.

nine Don't shower or bathe for as long as you can stand yourself.

ten Schedule dinner dates, meetings, and appointments your spouse needs to attend, but don't tell him or her until ten minutes before you need to be there.

eleven Don't buy any groceries.

twelve When your spouse leans in to kiss you, offer only your cheek.

Note: None of these are recommended for marriages you want to last.

One More Time, Please. Why Do Opposites Attract?

two

What counts in making a happy marriage is not so much how compatible you are, but how you deal with incompatibility.

—GEORGE LEVINGER

A LITTLE OVER FOUR YEARS AGO, my uncle died while scuba diving. It was a shock, and our entire family mourned. My aunt—who ran a bed-and-breakfast (B & B) in Alaska—asked if I could come up and help her the following summer for a few weeks. I accepted the invitation. The visit was incredible. I saw my first bald eagles, seals, whales, and puffins in the wild. I woke up early in the morning to pick fresh berries for scones to serve the guests. I explored Sitka, Alaska.

When my aunt invited me for a second summer, I jumped at the chance to return. I followed a similar routine. Eventually, word spread that I was a writer, and I was invited to sign books at a local church café. A number of people bought books that evening, including a 6'8" Norwegian, who purchased two. I didn't think much of it, but he did.

He was with a group of friends, and they invited me to play Pictionary after the signing. Over the next few weeks, I spent more time with them. It eventually became apparent—on the morning that he showed up at the B & B to cook a steak-and-eggs breakfast for me—that he was interested in being more than friends. Leif and I began dating. We went on walks, watched movies, and talked about everything under the sun. I asked tough questions, and he asked the same of me. By the time the summer came to an end, he asked if I would consider moving to Alaska to pursue a relationship.

The answer was simple: "No way!"

I was raised in Florida and Colorado, and he was asking me to move to southeast Alaska—the place where it rains 300 days a year. He had to be kidding.

He wasn't.

Over the next six weeks I prayed and thought about the decision. Leif happened to be in Seattle at the same time my mom and I were visiting for a relative's wedding, and she got to meet him. I'll forever remember her words: "You are a fool if you don't move up there."

I started packing.

Soon my car was loaded and I was on a ferry to take a house-sitting job in Alaska. Somewhere during the three-day ferry ride, Alaska became A-l-a-s-k-a. Now what I mean by that is that instead of saying Alaska as a quick word, it became A-l-a-s-k-a, where you overly enunciate every single letter as you're saying it. I made this switch to remind myself and everyone I knew what an enormous and rather chancy move this was for me.

Quick Tip: Take time to talk.

While I house-sat, Leif and I spent the winter, spring, and early summer really getting to know each other. I learned more about his history, family, childhood, values, beliefs, and faith. I saw him interact with friends, coworkers, and neighbors. Just to make sure he was the real deal, I would secretly ask people who knew Leif—but who didn't know we were dating—what he was really like. The responses were some of the kindest, most gracious words I have ever heard.

One overcast afternoon in July 2003, Leif invited me to go for a hike. We headed to one of our favorite trails. Less than a hundred yards into the hike, I discovered a long-stem red rose sitting beside the path with a handwritten note. A few yards later, there was another one. Then another one. For the next 2.5 miles, I collected 23 roses and notes. At the end of the path we came across a bench with a bowl, a thermos of warm water, another dozen roses, and a diamond ring. Leif bent down on one knee, asked me to be his wife, kissed me for the first time, and washed my feet. I said "Yes," and it was one incredible day!

During those months leading up to the big "Yes" moment, I put that poor man through the wringer. I challenged everything I could about him. I even threw a tantrum or two just to see how he would respond. I really wanted to know what he was made of, and more importantly, I wanted to know that I wasn't making a mistake. I was so afraid of making a bad decision—of choosing the wrong man. Though my own parents have been married for more than 30 years, I have watched countless couples—both old and young—go through painful separations and divorces, and it made me scared and cautious.

It made me so afraid that I came to a point—somewhere in those seven months—when there wasn't anything else I could poke or prod to find out more about Leif that I had to make the decision whether or not I was willing to take the chance.

The best way I can describe it is that I felt as though I were a person at a harbor having to pick a ship for a long journey. It was impossible to know what storms we would weather or what places we would visit. All I could do was choose the very best boat available. I had spent time examining the hull, engine, and cabins. I could look at the boat forever—inspecting every rope, cleat, and sail on board—but eventually I either had to select a boat and set sail or remain on the shore.

I chose to marry Leif, and it is one of the best decisions I have ever made. On September 20, 2003, Leif and I were married in my hometown of Steamboat Springs, Colorado, in a small Episcopal church. Friends and family flew in from all over the country, and though the ceremony was at 11 A.M., we stuck around and were able to enjoy being with all the guests until 11 P.M. It was a glorious day.

SURPRISE NO. 1

Expect an abrupt return to reality after your wedding. There's often an enormous high and a huge buildup to your wedding day. You're the center of attention. Gifts arrive nearly every day. You feel so special. Yet in what seems like overnight (and probably is), you're back to normal life. What goes up must come down. The good news is that eventually things do stabilize, and normal life does become normal again.

Leif and I spent the first few days after the wedding visiting people before returning to A-l-a-s-k-a. We needed a place to live before a five-month house-sitting stint began, so we rented a tiny apartment—that was really a hotel room—for five weeks. We nicknamed it "The Bat Cave" because it was so small. There was barely enough room for the king-sized bed for my large husband, a small table for my computer, a television, and a kitchenette. The bed became our dining room table, office, couch, loveseat, solarium, and the place we slept.

It was while living in the Bat Cave that I discovered my husband and I do things differently. In fact, we don't just have different ways of doing things: We are entirely different people. I knew this before we were married, but not in the same way you know it when you can't go to separate living quarters at the end of the day. It is the difference between taking a day sail and actually living aboard a boat. They're two different worlds.

Our differences pop up everywhere. I am intense. He is laid-back. I love a clean house. He recently asked me, "Why do we need Windex?" which for me is the equivalent of asking a Catholic, "Why do we need the Pope?" I like to exercise, eat healthy, and live an active lifestyle. My husband prefers to spend Saturday afternoons snuggling on the couch and eating pizza. I drink diet soda. He drinks regular. I like chicken breast. He prefers hamburger. I like warm weather. He prefers it cold.

Our differences manifest themselves in the way we go about doing some of the most basic things. If we buy a new item that requires assembly—whether it's an outdoor grill, electronic gadget, or cabinet from Ikea—I immediately begin putting it together. My husband, on the other hand, always reads the directions. When we cook, I avoid measuring cups and spoons whenever possible. It is simply a dash of this and a sprinkle of that. Meanwhile, my husband follows recipes with the precision of a nuclear scientist. When we pack for a trip, I am the typical Girl Scout—loaded down with every outfit (as if it's really going to snow in Florida), while my husband can fit everything into a backpack. Cleaning for Leif means that everything in the room is in straight piles, while I don't count something as clean unless it smells like Clorox, Tilex, or Pledge.

Quick Tip: Vacuum for no reason.

In the first few months of marriage, I remember thinking to myself, *There are so many differences. How are we going to make this work?* It is a thought that has visited several times since, and it's fairly common among young couples.

Hot Spot: The Kitchen

Nowhere were our differences more apparent than in the kitchen. After talking to a number of young couples, I'm convinced the kitchen is a universal hot spot for disagreement. I am blessed with a husband who loves to cook, but the way we go about cooking—from the amount of dishes and the spices we choose to slicing techniques—are completely different. Early in our marriage, I discovered this the hard way when I asked Leif to make a fruit salad.

> "It seems that most couples have this in common: The guys tend to second-guess themselves early—in the first year or two—and women a little later—the second through fifth year of marriage. Everyone seems to wonder *what if*. It's normal, but without a commitment that goes beyond emotions, it's too easy to give up and walk away. There should be no fear of wondering *what if* as long as there is a huge commitment to *what is*."
>
> —A DISCIPLESHIP PASTOR
> FROM ATLANTA, GEORGIA

I gathered everything together for him and placed it next to a cutting board. Slowly and steadily, he began carving up the fruit. Meanwhile, I made the salad, prepped the main course in the oven, prepared dessert, and set the table. When I was done, I looked over and noticed my beloved husband was just beginning to carve into a cantaloupe. He wasn't even close to being finished. I was exasperated. I didn't want to have to do all of the work for dinner, but I had never anticipated the fruit salad taking so long, and guests were scheduled to arrive in less than ten minutes.

I tried a less-than-graceful move of asking how the fruit salad was coming along.

"Just fine," Leif replied.

I looked at the small pile of sliced fruit in the bowl.

"You know the guests will be here soon?" I asked, slightly agitated.

"Yes," he said calmly, still precisely cutting each piece of fruit into exactly half-inch cubes.

Finally, I couldn't keep silent any longer. "Honey, what the heck is taking you so long? I've done the rest of meal. Look—the salad and dessert are made, the table is set, the main course is almost cooked. Can't you go any faster?"

"Well, of course I can go faster," he explained. "But then the slices won't be symmetrical."

"Aarrrgghhhh!" I cried out, stealing a line from the Peanuts comic strip. "It doesn't matter that it's symmetrical; it matters that it's done."

"Fine!" he said. "You ask me to do something, but then you don't let me do it. Why don't you just do it yourself?"

He headed into the living room. Rather than follow him, I attacked the remaining fruit with a vengeance. Why do all the worst fights have to happen three minutes before company arrives?

Ding-dong. They were already here.

Later that evening, after we put on our pseudo-smiley everything-is-fine-when-it's-really-not faces that every couple learns how to do within the first few hours of marriage, we had the opportunity to talk about what has become known as the Fruit Bowl Incident.

SURPRISE NO. 2

The biggest fights are usually over the littlest things.

Our conversation began with the humble and well-deserved apology I owed my husband. Over the next 45 minutes, I discovered things about him I never knew—like his fondness for precision. How could I have failed to notice that every slice of banana was equal in width? How did I overlook his natural appreciation for cooking? I had caught him watching the Food Network late at night at least a half dozen times. Why couldn't I see the obvious?

For Leif, cooking is an art form. For me, it's about putting food on the table. Through our discussion, I learned more about his childhood. When people came over to eat at his family's house, cooking together was part of the occasion. Guests would arrive and help slice and dice or barbecue. It made everyone feel closer and created an event rather than just a meal. In my family, having guests over meant everything was perfectly prepared and ready when the guests walked in. Guests weren't invited to cook because they were, well, guests. Both systems make sense depending on your upbringing, but it definitely was a cause for irritation for us.

Since the Fruit Bowl Incident, I am learning to become more open about having guests partake in the cooking, and my husband has finally agreed that the diameter of a slice of watermelon really doesn't affect the taste of the fruit salad. Although I will admit (when he's not in earshot), symmetry isn't such a bad thing after all.

That was just the Fruit Bowl Incident. What happens when we embark on the Purchase a House Adventure or the Have a Baby Phenomenon? If a fruit bowl can bring out differences in upbringing, style, and efficiency, what will happen when we have to make a big decision?

When Erynn, a 28-year-old, decided to purchase a house with her husband the first month of their marriage, she found the process to be quite stressful. "Everything moved

Moving Past an Argument

One of the biggest personal challenges about conflict isn't what you do with it, but rather what you do after it. After a disagreement or moment when I feel wronged, I tend to want to pout. Leif and I have developed an intentional system to battle this tendency. Whenever we have a disagreement or one of us feels wronged, the other person will apologize. Then the original person has to say three good things about the person who wronged them. The compliments range from "You're really cute" to "I love the way you make me feel when we're not having an argument." We've discovered that it's hard to be mad at someone you're encouraging and blessing verbally. It allows us to move past a disagreement more quickly.

ONE MORE TIME PLEASE

very quickly," she recalls. "But we talked a lot and through the discussion learned that we approach decision making and stress differently, and we were able to talk our way through so that we could understand each other and find the best way to move forward. With that and lots of prayer, it worked out beautifully."

Maybe home ownership and a fruit salad aren't that far apart after all. If we can learn to work through the little differences, then who says we can't use those same skills to work through the big ones? The fact is that it's in the little things that we learn how to resolve conflict, compromise, and gain a deeper understanding into each other's values and beliefs. Events like the Fruit Bowl Incident give us the opportunity to grow, so that when the Suddenly Laid Off Incident or the Won the Lottery Incident happen, we can handle ourselves a little better.

Sean, a 33-year-old who has been married for ten years, says one of the biggest differences he had with his wife was in decorating and maintaining their home. He describes himself as "fairly artistic" and "extremely compulsive" when it comes to neatness and cleanliness.

"My wife is no slob, but I am a chronic neat freak," he admits. "Unlike the typical male, I care very much about the wall color and wallpaper and bed sheet pattern. All of my guests were impressed with my bachelor pad—including the organization of closets and pantry. I even wiped down my baseboards once a week and vacuumed three to four times per week."

Sean and his wife struggled for the first few years of their marriage with their organizational differences, but over time Sean says his wife helped "heal" him. "It was a painful recovery," he says. "But she, being a master straightener and concealer, was able to help me relax (mostly) in a home that appears clean. The closets are divided with an imaginary wall that is clearly noted by the degree of clothes arranged on the hangers and those on the floor."

Quick Tip: Eat a burnt meal without complaint.

While cleanliness is still an issue the couple deals with, they have resolved it in some ways by assigning the responsibility of certain chores to each other according to their levels of pickiness. "I am not about to complain about the way the towels are folded if I do not take the time to fold them myself," he says. "She cannot complain about how I load the dishwasher if she does not take time to load it herself. When it comes to buying stuff to decorate, no purchases are made without mutual approval. This has actually caused us to spend more time together shopping and planning the look and feel of our house. My wife brags that her husband actually cares about home decor and quickly points out my contributions. But when it comes to cleaning and organizing, ten years later we are still learning to appreciate the effort, if not the end results."

Sean acknowledges that the differences between his wife and him have allowed him to grow, mature, and become more balanced. It's a lot like applying sandpaper. As two individuals come into a relationship and rub against each other with their individual quirks, tendencies, priorities, and values, they eventually wear each other down into smoother and gentler creations that can get along and work together more effectively.

What Was God Thinking?

Whenever I begin to get overwhelmed by the differences between my husband and me, I force myself to reflect on our similarities and what draws us together. I appreciate our mutual love for ministry, movies, and travel to beautiful places. We both share a passion for Jesus and enjoy writing and worship.

I also remember that our differences make us one incredible team. As a general rule, his strengths are my weaknesses and vice versa. Our characteristics actually complement each other. I can help motivate us to get things done on time, and my husband makes sure the job is done well. In the process I can grow impatient or I can choose to grow. Some days I still choose the former, but on a good day I choose the latter.

Even with the right perspective, there will always be things about each other that neither of us will ever understand. Like I don't understand why Leif loves to play Xbox for hours on end, and he doesn't understand my desire to live with a spot-free bathroom mirror. The differences between men and women are unexplainable at times.

As one husband who shall remain nameless (for his protection) said, "Girls—man, they're different. So many shoes, and they take so long to get ready just to go to the store. They get moody every three weeks, and it's really not my fault. And there's all that talking and talking. Where is the manual for girls?"

Even if there were a manual, I don't think any male would really be able to decipher it. Men and women are just wired differently.

Anna, who has been married for 42 years, highlights the differences she still has with her spouse, even after four decades of marriage, "I enjoy socializing and being with people and then having some downtime. My husband enjoys quiet and having his own space. I need people in my life more than Glen does. One of the most helpful things we did was a study on personalities. We viewed the video and teaching lessons by Florence Littauer called *The Personality Tree*. It put a lot of things into the right perspective for us, and we delighted in using it for small group ministry."

Here are some keys that Leif and I are slowly learning that can help in handling the differences you have with your spouse.

Be patient. It takes time to discover all your differences. You may bathe, sleep, eat, communicate, and carry yourselves differently. The way you love and prefer to be loved may be different. Your stress level when it comes to buying a car, stereo system, or bathing suit in the spring is probably going to be different. It's going to take time to learn all of those differences and figure out how they can make you a stronger couple. Give yourself (and your spouse) a break. Building understanding and unity takes time.

Discuss your differences. Rather than just acknowledge your differences, find out why your spouse does something a particular way. My husband likes to have the oil in our cars changed every three months. I prefer to do it every five or six months. After we discussed the issue, I discovered that he can actually tell a difference in the way a car runs when it has fresh oil, and he learned that I had read a report that says you can wait longer between oil changes. After our discussion, I agreed that he is welcome to change the oil in the car as often as he likes as long as I am not responsible for scheduling the appointment. Because we understand each other's reasoning, we can give each other more grace.

Recognize that your way isn't the only way. This one can be tough. You may be able to argue that your way is more efficient or effective, but that does not always make it right. For example, I was always taught to use a nonstick aerosol spray when I do any stovetop cooking. It saves calories and fat instead of using butter and makes cleaning the pan easier. My husband won't use nonstick spray on a nonstick pan. He says it's unnecessary. He is right. It's not the way I would do it, but it works. Remember that no matter what you're doing, you can learn to do it in a new way.

Learn from your differences. You can either be repelled or attracted to your spouse's differences. Depending on the day, you might be both. Ultimately, the choice is yours. Differences provide an opportunity to expand your understanding and perspective on life and possibly learn something new.

Give each other space. This can be challenging—particularly during the first season of a marriage. But it's important to allow each other time—each day—to be alone without having anyone's feelings hurt. This time apart will allow each person to adapt, compromise, and even come to a balance while still allowing the other person to be different.

Quick Tip: Take time to listen.

Recognize that some things will never change. Your spouse made it this far doing things that way, so there is a good chance your spouse will keep right on surviving. If your spouse is a morning person, gives new definition to the word "busy," talks to every stranger everywhere you go, or makes procrastination a hobby, remember that things could be worse. Similar things could be said of you.

Don't take yourself too seriously. Marriage is fun. Life will still go on even if (<u>fill in the blank</u>) doesn't happen. Take time to enjoy each other the way you did when you were dating. It makes life so much more enjoyable.

Even if you are a morning person and he is a night owl, you prefer decaf and he prefers full throttle, you prefer chick flicks and he's forever wanting to see the latest James Bond, you can still make things work. Just remind yourself when you agree to go to a midnight action film with a triple shot latte that you are stepping outside your comfort zone. But isn't your spouse worth it?

Questions for Reflection

1. How are you and your spouse different? How has your attitude toward those differences shifted since you've been married?

2. What have the differences taught you about yourself?

3. Has your relationship with your spouse given you insight or grace in dealing with other people who are different from you?

4. Why do you think God creates diverse people? Why do you think He puts them together for the rest of their lives?

The Scoop on the Bling Bling

Have you been caught admiring your own wedding ring?

29,303
The estimated number of jewelry stores in the United States. Jewelry stores sell wedding, engagement, and other rings and goods to lovers of all ages. Last February—think Valentine's Day—these stores sold $2.1 billion in merchandise. The only month sales were higher? December.

2266
The estimated number of jewelry manufacturing establishments in the United States. *

Looking for Love in All the Right Places

Two places in the United States have the name Valentine: Valentine, Nebraska (population 2820), and Valentine, Texas (population 187).

Nine places in the United States have the word "love" in their name, the largest of which is Loveland, Colorado, with more than 50,000 residents. If you're looking for a littler love, you can visit any of the following: Lovejoy, Georgia; Loves Park, Illinois; Lovelock, Nevada; Love Valley, North Carolina; Loveland, Ohio; Loveland Park, Ohio; Loveland, Oklahoma; and Lovelady, Texas.*

FOOTNOTE

* (Taken From: www.census.gov/Press-Release/www/2002/cb02-76.html)

* (Taken from: www.factfinder.census.gov/servlet/BasicFactsServlet)

Mirror, Mirror on the Wall— What Marriage Reveals About You

three

> *The real transforming work of marriage is the twenty-four-hours-a-day, seven-days-a-week commitment. This is the crucible that grinds and shapes us into the character of Jesus Christ.*
>
> —GARY THOMAS

WHEN YOU MARRY SOMEONE, YOU MARRY their struggles, past hurts, values, priorities, weaknesses, and strengths. They marry yours. While it's easy to place all the focus on your spouse, you may be surprised to discover how many of your own issues begin to surface.

During the first few months of my marriage, I struggled with an issue I had never faced before: self-hatred. That term sounds dark and ugly, and after living under its weight I can truly say it is as cruel as it appears. I had never faced this issue before I was married, and I had no idea where it came from, but I found myself being overly harsh and critical with myself. When I replayed a situation or the day's events in mind, all I could see was where I had made mistakes, said the wrong thing, and responded in the wrong way. I felt like a failure. While everything was wonderful—including my work, my husband, and our life together—I was extremely disappointed in myself. Yet I didn't know where it was coming from or what to do to change my thought pattern. I began to pray. I asked God to show me its source and how to overcome it. I shared this rather intimate struggle with my husband and asked him to pray both with me and for me.

The answer and freedom came several months later from a rather unexpected source. I was attending a Christian conference, and one of the sessions offered a personality assessment. I had taken personality tests before: the ones that determine whether you're an introvert or extrovert, leader or follower, otter or golden retriever. But I had never taken this particular test. I faithfully answered the questions and filled out the corresponding charts. Unlike the others, this one included two graphs: One revealed who I thought I should be and the other revealed who I actually was. I looked at the graphs side by side and discovered that they were the complete opposite of each other. The graph of my true personality was everything I knew myself to be, and I was content with that assessment. The graph of what I felt I had to be revealed everything that drove me into a state of discontent and eventually self-hatred. I realized that since I had gotten married, I had drawn an imaginary picture in my mind of what I was supposed to be. To be honest, it was completely unreasonable because it wasn't who God made me. It was a compounding cycle—the more I tried to become who I was not, the more frustrated I became with who I really was as a person.

Quick Tip: Play with your spouse's hair.

God uses all kinds of things to set people free, but in this case He used the results of a personality test to speak truth—His truth—into my life. I walked out of that workshop a new woman. Whenever a self-defeating thought has tried to rear its ugly head since, I have been able to remember those two graphs and know that God has designed me perfectly according to His plan.*

Not all of the issues that develop or emerge with marriage are resolved as quickly or easily as my struggle with self-image. Others take a lot longer.

Wrestling with Insecurity

Something about marriage naturally brings personal issues to the surface and forces you to dig up all kinds of things until you get to the root of the problem. You may find wounds from childhood, abuse from authority figures, personal mistakes, and poor choices finally catching up with you. Without the slightest intention, your spouse can act like a mirror showing you the innermost parts of your soul.

SURPRISE NO. 3

Issues that lay dormant when you were single tend to surface after you marry.

One of the biggest issues I've carried around with me over the years is an issue with my weight. I was put on my first diet when I was nine years old, and I've never fully recovered. I've tried everything from the grapefruit diet to eating cabbage soup for a week. I even did Atkins for 40 days last spring. I lost two pounds. I read about the South Beach diet and lost three. Maybe I should stick to reading about diets.

FOOTNOTE

* Leif had mentioned this word of truth to me months before. I guess God hadn't prepared me to hear that truth at that point, but thankfully I believe the change is permanent.

I used to fantasize that when I got married the issue with my weight would suddenly disappear. I would have a man who loved me for who I was and loved my body for how it was shaped. While living with an overly affirming, gracious husband has certainly helped, the battle scars of a lifelong struggle with food can't be erased by one person, even if your spouse thinks you look great 24/7. Leif's compliments and encouragement help, but I'm bringing years of emotional and mental baggage into our relationship. I have to face those every time we go to the beach, step into a hot tub, or unpack the summer clothes.

Recently, we were watching a show where a young gal was wearing some form-fitting summer outfit, and Leif asked me, "Why don't you wear something like that?"

"Because we live in Alaska, where the high is 60 degrees," I responded. "When we live in Florida—you got it."

I was only telling a half-truth, because living in the Sunshine State would only shed more light on my self-conscious frame. Though I have prayed regularly and read six more diet books even after the drop-three-pounds-a-diet-book phenomenon quit working, I still struggle with my weight and self-image. Only now I don't carry the struggle alone. My husband carries it with me. Sometimes this is helpful, as he challenges and encourages me. Sometimes it hurts, as I want to feel as beautiful as he sees me.

Everyone brings different baggage into a marriage. Ralph, who has been married 15 years, says that shortly after his wedding ceremony issues of insecurity and jealousy began to emerge. He was so insecure about himself that he couldn't believe someone could really love him.

He also discovered that his years of dating had affected his ability to trust anyone. "When you're dating, if you see someone you like who is different from what you have, you switch, or someone else leaves you for someone better," he observes. "In marriage, it is

Quick Tip: Read the Bible together.

forever—just the two of you—and no one else. That was a hard concept to grasp and also to believe that you were someone else's final and best choice they will ever want to make."

Marriage has a way of making all kinds of insecurities rise to the surface. You may struggle with your worthiness to be loved or become aware of other issues that have lived in the recesses of your life for years. Kate, a 26-year-old who has been married for less than a year and a half, says that marriage forced her to become more vulnerable than she had ever been with anyone.

"I really struggled with being overly sensitive," she says. "Everything from my appearance, dress, cooking, and interaction with others became a performance in my mind that I felt I could never quite pull off. I would read into things my husband said and interpret them—usually falsely—into something negative against me."

She says her actions and reactions were based on terrible fear: being discovered and then rejected. "I feel I have come a long way in this area—growing in my security and acceptance in Christ. As our marriage has grown, I have been able to let go of many of my insecurities due to my husband's persistent encouragement. He repeats often, 'I choose you.' I will never tire of hearing that and have begun to believe him. He has improved in verbally complimenting me, which greatly boosts my confidence."

In addition to her husband's support, Kate has clung to the Scripture: "If God is for us, who can be against us?" (Romans 8:31). Over time this verse has become a cornerstone in the foundation of her confidence. In addition, she has begun to internalize the praise found in Proverbs 31:11-12: "Her husband has full confidence in her and lacks nothing of value. She brings him good, not harm, all the days of her life."

Kate admits that this growth has not come without a cost. "I regret unnecessarily draining my husband by my deep insecurities and lack of confidence. I drove him to pep talking me into believing

I do have worth after all—even if I mess up repeatedly—and that he loves me regardless and chose me deliberately. I know it has depleted his love tank."

Kate realizes that there is no way her husband can have full confidence in her if she doesn't have any in herself. Ultimately, this security must come from God and her belief that she has been chosen by God as well.

SURPRISE NO. 4

The past never goes away.

Wrestling with Your History

Either your past or your husband's past may become a bigger issue than you anticipated. Marriage can act like a magnification mirror. It can make small blemishes look huge.

Kara, a recent newlywed, says one of the challenges she has faced stems from a combination of her family's background and her husband's past. "My father has disowned me, and my brother keeps waffling back and forth on whether he wants a relationship with me or not," she explains. "This has allowed me to work through feelings of abandonment and mistrust toward men."

She describes her husband as "more wonderful than she could begin to describe" and "the most faithful man I know," but reminders of his past marriage and a previous dating relationship have been challenging.

"Though I know that both relationships were abusive to him, I struggle with thoughts that there were other women besides me," she explains. "Neither woman is a threat, but reminders that are not so easy to forget or ignore still blare at the most inopportune times. The first thing I have done to work through this is to acknowledge every time this comes up that the enemy only wants to destroy something that was set in place by God. I am also trying to be more open about my feelings with my husband so that he can be aware of what I am struggling with and can help reassure me."

Kara is hopeful that as she continues to grow in her marriage, she will learn even more that she can trust her husband.

Like many couples, Anna also struggled with her past. She came from a very different kind of family than her husband. "My parents were not Christians and had not wanted children. I was the second oldest of four daughters," she says. "My father was an alcoholic. My grandmother raised us during our younger years. Eventually, my mother took responsibility and did her best to make a home for us. My father's alcoholism opened the door for many added problems and heartaches."

Anna says that she had to address the feelings of abandonment and rejection and the issues of abuse from her past. "I subconsciously thought my husband was going to make up for all the areas of my life that had been out of kilter. These unrealistic expectations set me up for disappointment."

Anna realized she had to take a serious look at who she was, why she felt the way she did, and how her feelings were affecting her relationship with her husband. "It came down to taking responsibility for who I am and for the choices that I make, whether in action or attitude," she says. "As the barriers of bitterness and resentment were peeled away, my relationship with the Lord and with my husband grew to new levels of intimacy. God has been so faithful and gracious and loving in the process. I am learning that my choice of attitude in any given situation can make a big difference in our marriage relationship."

Wrestling with Jealousy

Jealousy can be another issue that manifests itself—for both men and women. Newlyweds can be caught off guard by those who attract their spouse's attention even after they're married.

Quick Tip: Put on your spouse's favorite CD.

One young newlywed woman admits, "I have had to let go of [becoming jealous] because there are beautiful women all over the place. I am learning to believe my husband's repeated statements that he chose me and loves me and thinks I am beautiful. I have learned to be honest with him about how I feel in this area and even challenged him to keep a true eye. He has thanked me for the accountability, and it has drawn us closer together."

Ultimately, she says her security is in God. "The commitment my husband made to me in our vows is growing," she adds. "We are all susceptible to weakness, and this keeps me persistent in prayer for my husband." Through this challenge she says she is able to trust her husband and is receiving a bonus: She's deepening her ability to trust in God Almighty.

SURPRISE NO. 5

Jealousy doesn't disappear when you get married.

Wrestling with Other Issues

Marriage brings all kinds of issues to the surface—both large and small—because you can't do things the way you've been doing them. You have to coexist with another human and that requires compromise. Suddenly you can't hit snooze 15 times without waking someone else up who is still trying to sleep a little more. You can't leave the toilet seat up—unless you want to be awakened by the 4 A.M. yelp from your wife, who unknowingly sat down too far. You can't do things your way all the time.

One newlywed woman described her level of patience as being a big challenge. Known for jumping to conclusions, she found herself shortchanging her husband by not taking the time to really listen to him. She is learning to stop herself, be patient, and hear and see the whole picture before reacting and, more importantly, responding to her spouse.

Meanwhile, her patience has been tried as she learned to incorporate another person's agenda, work speed, ideas, rate of discovery, and inspiration. "When I want this or that done *now*, and my husband has a different idea of a priority, I am still learning to let it go, not begin nagging and trying to convince—it only makes things worse—and pray about it," she says. "After doing this, I often come to realize its insignificance anyway."

If you are like us and other married couples, don't be surprised to find yourselves wrestling with shadows from your childhood, previous relationships, abusive situations, and heartaches. In the past you may have been able to deal with issues on your own—in your apartment, your own house, or your own room—just you and God. Marriage requires you to involve a third party, and that can be tough when all you want to do is go into the corner, lick your wounds, and allow God to slowly heal them. The good news is that God is actually using your spouse to bring issues to the surface that you've been trying to hide from and run from for years. Maybe the new mirror God's installed in your life isn't so bad after all.

Questions for Reflection

1. What has your marriage taught you about your past and your spouse's past?

2. In what ways has God used your marriage to mature you?

3. What issues from your past need to be faced so you can have a better future together?

The (Seemingly) Eternal Change-Your-Name Checklist for Brides

___Driver's license

___Social Security Administration

___Immigration

___Passport

___Credit cards

___Frequent flyer memberships

___Buying clubs (Sam's Club/Costco, etc.)

___Employers

___Tax forms

___Bank accounts

___ Checks

___Insurance

___Vehicle registration

___Voter registration

___Mortgage company

___Landlord

___College/alma mater/student loans

___Retirement plan, including pensions, 401K, IRA

___Mailing lists

___Luggage tags

The Identity Crisis—Who Am I Now?

four

*God has made us
what we are.*

—EPHESIANS 2:10 NCV

FOR SOME WOMEN, CHANGING THEIR LAST NAME is as easy as changing their hair color. They embrace their husband's last name as if it were second nature. For other women, even Christian women (gasp!), it's a lot more difficult.

I was one of those women.

While truly in love with Mr. Leif Aaron Oines, I was less than eager to assume his last name. I had my reasons. First and foremost, for the seven years preceding our wedding date I had established myself as an author and speaker. I was known as Margaret Feinberg. To change my name meant parting with not only a name, but also a brand. Think about it for a second. If you saw two books—one written by Margaret Oines and another written by Margaret Feinberg in a bookstore, would you think the same person wrote them? Neither would anyone else.

I also didn't want to give up the name Feinberg because it represented something important to me: my heritage. I have fond memories of my Jewish grandmother, who escaped from Poland shortly before World War II, made matzo ball soup with the best of Jewish women, and told me stories of her childhood. Letting go of that part of my life was just too hard, especially since I am the last Feinberg—with no brothers—in this branch of the family tree. I made a compromise. Legally, I am Margaret Ann Oines, but for all professional purposes, I am Margaret Ann Feinberg.

The whole process of deciding on a last name has been a huge struggle for me. I'm not overwhelmed with joy over the name Oines. I know. I'm a terrible person. A terribly honest person. It's difficult for people to know how to pronounce, and it's one of those names that will get you picked on when you're on the elementary school playground (and that's according to my husband). If you had one of *those* names, you know what he's talking about. Not that Feinberg was always a load of fun. I felt a little better after I noticed some friends who were taking on the new last names of Funkerburger, Oob, and Dick. Oines didn't sound so bad after all. For one brief moment I dreamed of starting a support group for people who draw snickers, smiles, and "excuse me?" responses whenever they share their name. At least I was in good company. *

SURPRISE NO. 6

Changing your name may be a bigger change than you expected.

If you or someone you know has struggled with a name change, there's probably a reason or two. You may have always wanted to keep your name. It may carry a certain value to you—whether it's

* On the flip side, if you had one of these names and you get to trade it in for something people can easily spell and pronounce, and it doesn't describe or rhyme with a body part—you're one lucky individual!

independence, heritage, or freedom. You may have made a promise to a parent or sibling. You may have a professional reason for keeping your name. You may have tried alternatives, like Feinberg-Oines, and discovered they just won't roll off anyone's tongue, no matter how you try to twist it. Or you may have just grown so attached to your name you don't want to let it go.

Whatever the reason, you may decide to keep your last name or a portion of it. In some Christian circles, you may find yourself a little less than popular for your decision. The most important factor is that you and your spouse agree on your decision. For a lot of men, the issue of the wife assuming a new last name is important.

"I think for a lot of conservative guys—like me—it's a really big issue," my husband, Leif, explains. "If you're going to choose to spend your life with me, then that includes all of me—my name too."

Whatever decision you decide to make, take some time to discuss and reflect upon your decision. And remember that if you change your mind, you can always make another name change.

Kara, who has been married for just a few months, says that when it came to changing her last name, she experienced a sort of identity crisis. "It wasn't that I didn't want to change my last name," she explains. "And it wasn't even difficult that half the world knew me by my maiden name and the other half knew me by my married name. The crisis came when I had to prove I was the person I said I was—over and over again."

> **Tips to Changing Your Name**
>
> - Use your new name consistently, if at all possible.
> - Let friends, family, and coworkers know which name you prefer.
> - Get several certified copies of your marriage certificate and carry one with you.
> - Change your name on all of your identification.
> - Be gracious to those who unintentionally call you by your previous name.

Pulling out all the documentation to prove that you're married became exhausting for Kara. She started to feel frustrated every time she was asked for a birth certificate or driver's license.

The struggle was compounded when Kara realized that her husband didn't have a clue as to what she was going through. "Not only did he not have to change his name, but we kept his post office box for our mail," she explains. "He didn't even have to change his address!"

So Much More than a Name

Kara isn't alone when it comes to struggling with issues of identity after marriage. Many recent marrieds find themselves facing issues of identity after they say "I do," and they aren't always tied into a surname.

Leslie, a 31-year-old who has been married for nearly three years, says she didn't struggle with identity issues during the first year of marriage, but found herself struggling later on with her status as a married person.

"I'm a very busy and social person, and it took a while for me to realize that part of my frustration was that I was trying to keep up with the things I was able to do when I was single and kept getting frustrated or feeling like I was failing because I couldn't," she says. "Being single was a lot of fun for me, but being married is a completely different kind of fun. So basically I had to learn to bury the single me because it is no longer that season in my life. Allowing myself to get frustrated over missing it was interfering with the new season of being married."

Like many recent marrieds, Leslie says that while she wouldn't change her marital status for anything, she still misses the social aspects of her single lifestyle—the extended times with friends and group movie nights.

Quick Tip: Take an afternoon and fly a kite together.

With all the changes that happen during the first few months and years of marriage, it's not unusual to struggle with the change, especially if you've waited until you were older to get married. Many men and women find themselves living a content and full life as a single. When the right person comes along, they joyfully get married but discover a longing for some of the freedom and relationships that only the single life can afford.

"In a lot of ways it's similar to grieving the death of a loved one," Leslie says. "It's a big change when you've been single for so long."

It can be quite a challenge to establish your identity apart from your family.

Family Ties

Another way identity issues manifest themselves is through our relationships with our family. This is particularly true of individuals who are extra close to their families.

Renee, a 26-year-old newlywed, says she entered marriage still feeling identified with her parents and siblings. "I grew up very close to them and feel more loyal to them much of the time than I do with my new husband," she says. "It took me about a year to realize the conflict of loyalties and need for a change. I love my husband and knew I had left my father and mother to be united in a new way with him."

While Renee didn't overly involve her parents in unnecessary details of her marriage or struggles, she says they still held the first place in her mind. This was most noticeable during the holidays, when she would always insist on being with her parents. "There would be times when I would have a technical or mechanical question and would call my dad to inquire," she recalls. "I now know this hurt my husband and did not help empower him to be the leader of our new family. It has taken me a while to realize the depth of this new union."

Whatever identity issues your marriage may help uncover, knowing yourself in relation to your spouse and having your identity rooted in Christ is essential. One day you may become a parent or a grandparent, change professions, or live in another country. All of these are potential changes in your life, but the core of who you are—and who Christ made you to be—will remain the same.

> "The more you reaffirm who you are in Christ, the more your behavior will begin to reflect your true identity."
>
> —DR. NEIL ANDERSON

How do you get a grasp on your identity now that you're married? First, you need to know who you are as an individual. What are your likes and dislikes? What are your passions? What do you enjoy doing in your free time? If time and money weren't an object, what would you want to do with your life? Pull out a few sheets of paper and begin making some lists. Record your ideals, values, and preferences.

Once you've made your lists, take some time to reflect on them. What do they say about you? Which of your interests have been mentioned to you by people you know? Maybe someone commented that you're great with kids, good with money, or have a talent with singing.

If you haven't taken a personality test in a few years, it's probably time to take one—either in a book or online. Answer honestly and consider what the results say about you. In addition, you may want to take a spiritual inventory test to determine how you can best serve others with your spiritual gifts. These resources, combined with your personal lists, help draw a picture of you.

One of the things that has surprised me the most about marriage is how much my husband has taught me about myself. Because he has the opportunity to watch me 24/7 and observe how I respond and react to certain situations, events, and people, he can often provide insight into how I behave. For example, after a draining week he'll remind me that I need to avoid the tendency to overextend myself by committing to more activities. He often asks questions that reveal when my motivations are fear- or guilt-driven. And he is able to encourage me to use the gifts that God has given me rather than step into areas that I'm simply not called. While Leif doesn't give me my identity, he helps me to see myself for who I truly am— a child of God.

And that is where our identity ultimately comes from. John 1:12 says: "But whoever did want him, who believed he was who he claimed and would do what he said, He made to be their true selves, their child-of-God selves" (MSG). More than a last name or a marital status or a profession, we are created as children of God and are invited to grow in our relationship with Him. As we mature and find ourselves established in the truth of what Christ and the Scriptures say we are, we'll find ourselves living out our true identity.

Questions for Reflection

1. If you had to change your last name, how easy or difficult was the decision? Have you talked to your spouse about your (or her) decision?

2. How has marriage challenged your identity?

3. What was it like to adapt to a married lifestyle? What things were easy to give up? What things were more difficult?

4. What does your identity look like without God?

five | Great Expectations— What to Do When Your Spouse Isn't Fulfilling Them

You may ask how you can see your spouse as God does. This perspective comes only from prayer. The more I pray for [my wife], the more I see her as God sees her—through eyes of love and concern for her spiritual growth.

—DAVID G. BENNER

RAISED ON STORIES OF CINDERELLA AND SNOW WHITE, it's easy to imagine your future husband as being a Prince Charming of sorts. A man who will worship the ground you walk upon, give his undivided attention to you whenever you need it, understand your every motive and desire, and bring you flowers on a regular, if not daily, basis. He will never give you a cross look or an angry reply, will keep the house clean and the checkbook balanced without being asked, and will constantly think of romantic ways to shower you with his affection. Not only will Prince Charming anticipate your needs and moods and respond perfectly, he will shower you with unlimited kisses, hugs, and affection, never expecting anything in return. You'll get to live happily ever after. Please note: Real men need not apply.

Sometimes I think the world would be a better place without Meg Ryan and Tom Hanks in movies like *Sleepless in Seattle* and *You've Got Mail*. Okay, you're right, we really do need them in our DVD libraries, but they paint a portrait of love and romance that isn't realistic for the long haul. Meg manages to fall into Tom's loving arms at the end of both movies, but then we don't get to see the rest…the Sunday afternoons when all he wants to do is watch football and the big fight after she maxes out the credit cards for the third time. As a result, we are left to figure out what long-term love looks like on our own.

Beth and Nick, who have been married for more than three decades, were willing to talk about how Prince Charming expectations affected their relationship. When they were dating, Beth says she only saw the good things in Nick. "After we were married, I saw the feet of clay," she says. "No one could have lived up to [my expectations]. I got a wonderful man who was very much in love with me but also self-centered, who tried hard but always seemed to fall short. It wasn't his fault; it was mine."

It took her a long time to realize that feet of clay were the norm, not Prince Charming.

Nick says he wishes he would have known his wife was expecting a knight in shining armor. "I would have tried to be more like that," he says. "I assumed she knew exactly how flawed I was. I wish I knew she wanted to be more cherished and exactly what that meant to her."

Ever After is a movie, not real life.

Expecting a Candlelight Dinner

Have you ever thought to yourself, *Wouldn't it be great if I got home and my husband* _____ (fill in the blank: *had a candlelight dinner waiting for me, did the week's grocery shopping on his lunch break, cleaned the kitchen, or sent flowers "just because"*)?

Such imaginary tangents are easy and common among married women. They are also dangerous. They have a tendency to leave us feeling disappointed and frustrated when they are unfulfilled, and they're not fair to our spouse.

Sometimes our daydreams are sparked by a film, novel, or the latest *Inside Hollywood* exclusive, but they often come when we begin comparing our spouse and marriage to someone else's. Erynn, a newlywed, discovered how easily expectations could be formed while attending a church-sponsored women's retreat. The first morning Erynn and a friend were in their cabin putting things away when another cabin-mate came over and asked if her outfit seemed to fit and look okay.

"I looked up and found her in a very cute, very flattering pair of jeans and a feminine, trendy top—all with the store tags still attached," she recalls. "I was a little confused but told her I thought she looked great."

The woman explained that her husband had handed her a bag full of clothes when he dropped her off for the retreat. He wanted her to feel special, so he purchased her several new outfits.

Erynn and her friend agreed that was a thoughtful, sweet, and romantic thing for him to do. He had not only thought of the idea, but he also followed through and bought her complete outfits that looked fabulous on her. "As we left the cabin talking about it, I noticed that both my friend and I began to sound a little envious," Erynn says. "I know that right then we both were about to let ourselves think, *Why didn't my husband do something for me?* I had to stop and remind myself about how wonderful my husband is in so many ways, and that it is never fair of me to be disappointed if he isn't doing or saying things I see other men doing in their relationships. My husband doesn't leave me lacking in any area. There are lots of things that are unique to him that other men might not say or do."

Ultimately, Erynn says she wants to always focus on the gestures and encouragements that her husband does shower on her. "He is God's gift to me, and I want to always appreciate my special gift rather than find fault with it," Erynn says. "It takes conscious effort most of the time to control my expectations and keep them healthy."

The comparison trap is easy to fall into for anyone. At any given time, you have the mates of coworkers, friends, church leaders, and even in-laws with which to compare your spouse. Whether you're comparing your spouse to J. Lo, Brad Pitt, or the new neighbor two doors down, in one way or another almost all of them will shine brighter than your spouse at first glance. One may be more handy around the house, better equipped to handle finances, or more of a leader. Another may maintain a better physique, dress better, or act like more of a spiritual leader. When you fall into the comparison trap, you sow seeds of discontent into your marriage. Instead of focusing on what you've been given through your spouse, you see all the areas that are lacking. And if you look too long, they grow bigger and darker until all you can see are faults and blemishes.

How do you change your mindset? First, by changing your mind. Ask God to give you fresh eyes to see the strengths of your spouse.

GREAT EXPECTATIONS—WHAT TO DO

Consider making a list. Then, throughout the next week, let your spouse verbally know the things you like. Affirm your spouse.

It is also important to remember that every strength has its weakness. The perfect spouse does not exist because everything you see that is appealing always comes with a cost. One of my husband's weaknesses is that he isn't very time conscious. He hates to be late, and yet he refuses to wear a watch because he finds them uncomfortable. At the root of this weakness, though, is a strength. My husband is very laid-back. He knows how to slow down and enjoy an afternoon or evening. Because he's not time conscious, he does an amazing job of being fully present with people, including me. In other words, when we're together, he's not distracted by projects, to-do lists, or the clock. I enjoy the benefit of his full attention, and I bask in it. If given the choice between a time-conscious personality and a relaxed, fully present disposition, I'd choose the latter every time. So when I get tweaked over his late arrival or his sudden dash off to a meeting, I remind myself that I'm still winning in the long run.

SURPRISE NO. 9

It's not against the law to call your husband and ask him to buy you flowers.

I also battle unrealistic expectations about my spouse by becoming open and vulnerable about my needs and desires. On a recent flight home, I really needed Leif to be at the airport waiting for me with flowers in hand. I spent half of one of the flights daydreaming about my Norwegian giant holding a bouquet when I stepped off the plane. I wondered if he could somehow hear my thoughts from thousands of miles away. Maybe, because I had been away for ten days, he would think of it on his own. Or if I prayed hard enough, maybe God would plant the idea in his mind. I dreamed. I fantasized.

Then I pulled a Dr. Phil and got real.

Quick Tip: Give your spouse a foot massage.

I called my husband and left a message on his voicemail asking him to pick up some flowers for my arrival. When I hung up the phone, I felt a slight twinge of reality—had I taken the magical romance out of the moment? Maybe a little, but when I landed, Leif was waiting with a big smile, a warm embrace, and a fresh bouquet. When we talked about it afterward, he said he was thrilled that I had the courage to call him and make the request, and in the end we were both very happy.

Expecting Your Best

The expectations that you carried into your marriage aren't all about your spouse. They may have come from books you read, relationships you observed from a distance, or from your own upbringing. Maybe your mom always had a hot meal on the table at the end of the day or your dad always took out the trash. Maybe one of your parents always took care of the garden or lawn, managed the finances, or handled the upkeep on the house. Now you think you should be able to do the same as your same-gender parent simply because you grew up watching them do it.

SURPRISE NO. 10

Your life with your spouse is going to look different from life you experienced as a child.

Some of the toughest expectations people face in a marriage are the ones they place on themselves. If you have ever studied Proverbs 31 and believed that this ultra superwoman—the ideal Christian wife and mother—is supposed to be you 24/7, you're going to have a tough road ahead of you. You simply can't do it all every moment of every day.

The standard for many women is their mom; for many men, it's their dad. While parents can serve as role models, it is important to remember that we live in a different day and age than they did. We face different job pressures, financial strains, and demands. The life you live with your husband may very well look different from the one you grew up enjoying, but that doesn't mean that it's not healthy, satisfying, or pleasing to God. If you are struggling with expectations you have placed on yourself or your spouse, then take some time in prayer to reflect and offer them to God. Ask Him which expectations are realistic and which are forcing to you carry a weight that is simply too much to bear.

Expecting Your Spouse to Be Just like You

One of the biggest expectations many newlyweds carry into the relationship is that their spouse will respond or react in the same way they do.

Miguel, a 23-year-old who has been married for a year, says that expectations over entertaining guests became a point of conflict in his marriage. "When I bring visitors home—guy friends—sometimes she will not acknowledge their presence by saying 'Hello' or 'Hey, how are you?' or at least greet them in some form," he says. "I grew up in Brazil and my family—like most families in Brazil—is very warm and full of hospitality. In fact, in Brazil it is very impolite for you to be in a room with someone you don't know and not greet them with a kiss. If I brought a friend over, my mom would come and kiss his or her cheek, give them a hug, and usually go make some kind of food to present to the guest while they're visiting. I think sometimes I put those expectations on my wife and compare her with my mom, and when [my wife] doesn't respond the way I feel like she should, it makes me mad."

Miguel says he has to remind himself that he is in another culture and that his wife has grown up in a different family. He says the way they work on this issue is simply by talking about how they grew up and their cultural differences. "As we understand each

Quick Tip: Let your spouse have the window seat when you fly together.

other's background, it really helps us be more sensitive to how we respond to each other's actions," he says. "This was a bigger challenge in the first few months of our marriage than it is now."

You may find yourself expecting your spouse to know how to do a hundred things—from brewing a cup of coffee to ironing a pair of pants to organizing a desk—just like you. It sounds silly now, when you think about it—expecting another human being with an infinite number of complexities to do something the same way that you do. And such thinking is limiting—not only for your spouse—but also for you because you limit your ability to learn to do something in a new way.

One of the greatest tools to battle expectations—whether you put them on yourself or your spouse—is teachability. When you go through a situation with an attitude that is humble and willing to learn, then you place yourself in a no-lose situation. There is always something you can get out of it. With an expectation of learning something new, you probably will.

Questions for Reflection

1. What are some of your husband's weaknesses? What are the strengths that naturally accompany those weaknesses?

2. What can you do to change your mindset about your spouse's weaknesses?

3. Do you have any expectations about yourself that you carried into your marriage? Which of these have you been able to fulfill? Which have remained unfulfilled?

4. Which of the expectations you've placed on yourself as a newlywed are simply unrealistic? What will it take for you to let go of them?

six

Can You Hear Me Now? Reconnecting in a Disconnecting World

*No couple who marries
is ever compatible. It's
a lifelong process of
becoming compatible.*

—H. Norman Wright

I CANNOT REMEMBER EXACTLY HOW LONG it was after we were married that my husband needed to travel for work, but I remember that he was going to have to be gone for three days. Not just any three days, mind you, but three whole days and three whole nights. I took the news fairly well the first go-round. I began dreaming of all the things I could do. I would have dinner with single friends, tackle the much-delayed project of putting together a wedding photo album, and watch some teary-eyed, sappy movies while eating too much popcorn and chocolate. My mind started to whirl. I calculated everything I could fit into the time frame and figured I could get at least a dozen or more things done I had been meaning to do. This was going to be a great three days—one big, long party—and I was going to make the most of the solo time.

At least that's what I thought when he first told me.

As his departure date approached, I began to have second thoughts. Three days began to seem like a long time. After all, we had just been married, and we had never been apart that long. Three days suddenly seemed like a really, really long time. The day before my husband left, I found myself clinging to his side. Whether we were reading a book or watching television, I was draped over him like a wool blanket. When he went to run an errand, I was in the car beside him, my hand clutching his right knee. When he went to the bathroom, I was right outside the door. Pathetic, I know. It didn't feel like my husband was leaving for a few days; it felt like he was leaving forever.

I still don't know what happened. A year before I had been a highly independent single woman. In less than 12 months I had been transformed into a needy married woman. What happened to the independence? What happened to the freedom of the solo life? What happened to the zing of being on your own? I didn't know, and frankly, I didn't care. My husband was leaving for his first work trip since we had been married, and I didn't like it.

SURPRISE NO. 11

Saying goodbye is tough to do. Yeah. Yeah. Yeah.

I woke early in the morning to say goodbye. It was 4:00 A.M., and though I was crazy-in-love there was still enough sanity to tell me that it wasn't reasonable to go to the airport with him when he would just have to disappear behind security anyway. So I stood in my pajamas clinging to my husband like a child clings to her father when he's about to take a trip. Finally, the time came to let go, and I mustered the inner strength to release him into the great unknown.

I climbed back into bed and fell asleep. When my alarm went off at 7:00, I was officially entering my first day on my own. Despite the fear and anxiety of the previous day, I decided I was going to party like a rock star. I went to the store and bought some comfort food, scheduled dinner with some friends, and decided to work late—which for me is a real treat. Okay, I admit that I called my husband at least four times throughout the day, but by the time I tucked myself into bed that night, I was content.

The second day was a bit bumpier. I tried to roll out of bed with that same *carpe diem* attitude, but somewhere between lunch and getting off work, it fell into the recesses. Nonetheless, I stuck to the plan: chick flicks, popcorn, and chocolate. I remember thinking that it was fun, but kind of like hollow fun, because I was not with my best friend. I couldn't make it through the first film without pausing the DVD, picking up the phone, and letting him know how much I missed him.

It was all downhill from there.

I realized I was alone, and I felt very alone. I lay in bed thinking that it was not as warm and cozy when he was not there. I actually missed seeing his cereal bowl left in the sink in the morning— an act that usually annoys me. By nightfall I was sitting on the couch staring at the television and counting down the hours until his plane landed. So much for the party; this wasn't the rock star single life I had dreamed about.

When I met my husband at the airport, my heart sang. I wrapped my arms around his broad shoulders, planted a big kiss on his lips, and determined never to let him go again—at least until the next business trip.

Quick Tip: Send flowers to your spouse at work.

We headed home. I was no longer alone. My best friend was back. As I nestled into his warm arms that night drifting off to sleep, I thought nothing could be better.

Little did I know what was coming the next day.

A Sense of Disconnectedness

Though my husband still had to go to work the next day, we spent a few moments together before he left. When he came home after work, we desperately wanted to spend time with one another, but we had already committed to getting together with friends. We talked for a half hour or so before bed, but because he was exhausted and we still had one more workday left in the week, sleep was a priority.

By the time Friday night came, I couldn't help but feel a sense of disconnectedness with Leif. It's hard to describe. We spent the evening chatting and finally settled into a movie, but it was like we were exchanging information rather than having a real heart-to-heart conversation. Even though we had talked on the phone more than a dozen times during his trip, both of us were still dripping with details about the week's events and incidents. When we finished talking, we began to watch a movie together. But for some reason I was sitting on the opposite end of the couch. He asked me to move closer to him, and I did, but something was out of sync.

Saturday rolled around and we found ourselves making breakfast. Instead of cooking together, we were largely in each other's way. I didn't like the eggs he prepared for me, and he wasn't too crazy about the slightly burnt bacon. When we tried to talk about things, there was an unnatural awkwardness. It was as though neither of us knew what to say, and when we said something, it was either incorrectly expressed or interpreted.

Quick Tip: Take dance lessons together.

I felt like I was on the cell phone advertisement where the man asks, "Can you hear me now?" and all I could hear from my husband was, "Do you want to bow?" I misheard things he said throughout the day, and finally we reached the point where we had to stop and ask each other, "What's going on here?"

We each expressed our varying degrees of disconnectedness. We acknowledged that we were still head over heels in love with each other, but in a mere 72 hours we had managed to return to the independent routine we had when we were single.

We decided to do the activities that made us connect in the first place when we were dating. We took a long walk. We enjoyed lunch together. We snuggled on the couch. We talked. We shared. We listened. We prayed. Oh yeah, and we had sex. By the next day, we were connected again.

Dealing with Disconnectedness

Since that first business trip, I have become a little more used to my husband leaving for work. He has become used to me taking trips too. Traveling is part of our job requirements. When we can afford it, we make every effort to take the trip together. When doing so is beyond reach, we try to make the best of the situation. Of course, it doesn't help that we only spent six days together in the entire month of May (our ninth month of marriage). Being apart from each other for three days (or more) still isn't fun, but I have discovered that it isn't the end of the world, either. It provides time to catch up with friends, work on projects, spend longer times praying and studying the Bible, and have some much-needed alone time.

SURPRISE NO. 12

It's far too easy to get disconnected from your spouse.

The sense of disconnectedness hasn't been as easy to handle. No matter how many times one of us travels for work, we still struggle with a sense of being disconnected after the trip. Sometimes I struggle with it before he's gone because quietly I'm upset that he's leaving and my comfy little married world is getting shaken.

It's not just business trips, though, that can lead to a sense of disconnectedness. It can happen to any couple, anytime, when either spouse gets too busy to connect with the other. A bunch of extra meetings, a change in work schedule, an illness, and even commitments with good intentions can lead to a feeling of disconnectedness.

Anna, a 27-year-old who recently celebrated her second anniversary, says a change in her work schedule caused a serious sense of disconnectedness in her relationship with her husband. "During February we each were scheduled to work on opposite days. We didn't have the same day off together for nearly a month and a half. During that time, we even took a ministry trip together with a youth group, but we were so busy ministering to others that we didn't have more than ten minutes together during the trip to talk. We went through a time of disconnectedness afterward. We just couldn't communicate, and I found myself angry over the littlest things. It took time intentionally hanging out together and reconnecting to get us back to the healthy place we were in before things got so busy. It's awesome to want to serve God and build relationships with others, but we've really got to guard our time together."

So even if you and your spouse don't travel a lot, you may find yourself dealing with a sense of disconnectedness. Fortunately, reconnecting with your spouse may not be as hard as you think.

Schedule time to spend together. If you're going to reconnect with your spouse, you're going to have to intentionally spend time together. That may mean saying no to meetings, dinners, parties, and events to spend time one-on-one. Set aside an entire day, or as much of a day as you can, to hang out and do what you both enjoy doing together. Sometimes that's watching a movie. Sometimes that's sitting on the couch lazing around all day.

Leif and I have learned that when one of us travels, we mark off the day before and after the other person leaves to spend the entire day together. Hopefully, those days fall on a weekend, but if they don't then we schedule the next full day off work to be together. We turn down invitations and commit to giving each other the time needed to reconnect.

Do the activities that connected you to your spouse in the first place. Every couple has activities that naturally bring them closer together. You or your spouse may enjoy a sport like hiking, rock climbing, swimming, or golfing together. You may like trying out a new restaurant, exploring back roads, or shopping together. You may prefer watching a movie, visiting a library, or playing a game together. Think back to when you were dating. What activities did you enjoy doing together? What activities do you enjoy doing now together? Part of reconnecting is sharing common experiences together, so carve out times to enjoy the activity and, more importantly, each other.

Take time to really listen. Miscommunication can quickly contribute to the sense of disconnectedness. You will find that your spouse will say one thing and you will hear something completely different. When you are in a time of disconnectedness, go out of your way to really listen to your spouse. Be sensitive of your location to them when you're talking. Repeat things back to them, if necessary, to make sure your understanding is

Activities You Enjoy as a Couple

___ Movies	___ Long walks
___ Volleyball	___ Eating lunch at a bistro
___ Cooking	___ Road trips
___ Television	___ Listening to music
___ Softball	___ Candlelight dinners
___ Cuddling	___ Volunteering
___ Other	

(Check all that apply and add a few of your own.)

complete. You may want to say, "What I'm hearing you say is

_____."

Have sex. While sex should not become the basis or the only way you reconnect, it is definitely part of the package. Becoming vulnerable and intimate can help you to naturally feel closer to your spouse.

Nurture the sense of connection. Once you've retrieved the sense of connection with your spouse, don't let it go. Intentionally do things that you know will bring a smile to your spouse's face. Keep carving out time to spend together and communicate.

One of the biggest things Leif and I have learned to do is to curb times of disconnectedness by establishing boundaries for our marriage and relationship. My husband and I both struggle to say no to others. We both want to be everything to everyone, but we also know that isn't possible and is not what God has called us to do. We are learning—step-by-step—to defend our time, carve out date nights, and make sure we have adequate time for each other before we become too involved in an event, outreach, or ministry opportunity. We have also learned—the hard way—that working together isn't always the same as being together. We may do a project together but still fail to connect.

SURPRISE NO. 13

You have to protect the time you have with your spouse in order to cultivate your marriage.

Depending on your schedule, you may need to set apart one day a week to be together. You may want to develop the habit of having a date night every week or schedule getaway weekends on a regular basis. Find out what works for you as a couple and make this time sacred. People, events, and activities will try to take back the hours you've set aside to be together, but these hours are worth protecting.

During those special times appointed for you two, practice being fully present with each other. In other words, quiet the cell phone, unplug the computer, and turn off the ringer on the home phone. Talk face-to-face rather than filling your time with activities. If you're distracted by a project or a to-do list, then make a note of what you need to do on a piece of paper and set it aside for later. Do whatever it takes to protect and guard your time to be together.

Questions for Reflection

1. Describe the last three times you felt disconnected from your spouse. Do you see a pattern in the causes of disconnectedness?

2. How did you reconnect with your spouse each time? What works for you as a couple?

3. What steps can you take to minimize times of disconnection in your relationship?

4. What do you need to do to be fully present when you're with your spouse?

Romantic Movies, Anyone?

On a lazy afternoon when you find yourself snuggling under a soft blanket with your spouse, why not put in a romantic movie for some good cuddle time? Here's a short list of recommendations:

Sleepless in Seattle (**1993**) How can you resist this Meg Ryan and Tom Hanks remake of an *Affair to Remember*?

An Affair to Remember (**1957**) This Cary Grant film follows a romantic tale that takes you to the top of the Empire State Building.

My Big Fat Greek Wedding (**2002**) This surprise blockbuster starring Nia Vardalos and John Corbett reminds us that there aren't any differences that can't be overcome.

Ever After (**1998**) This creative remake of the Cinderella story starring Drew Barrymore and Anjelica Huston reminds us of what romantic movies are supposed to be like.

Breakfast at Tiffany's (**1961**) Audrey Hepburn and George Peppard star in this classic, timeless film based on the novella by Truman Capote.

Titanic (**1997**) Who can forget Leonardo DiCaprio and Kate Winslet stumbling upon romance on a fateful voyage?

Beauty and the Beast (**1991**) Belle reminds us that love can overcome any obstacle.

Casablanca (**1942**) This story of sacrifice, war, and love starring Humphrey Bogart and Ingrid Bergman will continue to be a favorite for generations to come.

If you are looking for a romantic film in a theater, visit www.comingsoon.net to read descriptions and view trailers of new and upcoming films.

What Did You Just Say? Dialing Up the Level of Communication

seven

Becoming married takes time. It doesn't just happen on the wedding day. The wedding is only the beginning of a relationship that can be expected to endure and grow.

—Douglas J. Brouwer

WHEN YOU LIVE TOGETHER, YOU GET TO KNOW someone in a whole new light. Several years ago I was visiting with a family for some weeks. I watched a pattern develop during my stay that changed the way I understood communication in marriage. Each night the father of the house would come home exhausted and slightly disgruntled from a long day at work. His wife would greet him at the door, kiss him on the cheek, and ask about his day, to which he would offer a one-word or short, one-sentence reply. Dinner was always ready on the table, and while the rest of the family would dialogue, the father was always a bit reserved and quiet.

After dinner everyone would go to their separate activities and projects and the husband would sit on the couch reading the paper. Eventually the wife would take a seat on the couch beside him. She wouldn't say anything. Just by being in his presence, something magical would happen. He would begin to open up and talk about his day. It usually started with a short sentence or observation, but within 15 minutes the husband and wife were engaged in a deep, meaningful, and connecting conversation. The wife had discovered the golden key to getting her husband to open up—simply sitting beside him quietly for a few minutes each evening—and as I sat on another couch with my nose discreetly nestled in a book, I knew I was witnessing one of the many miracles of marriage.

The importance of communication cannot be overstated. When communication is free, open, and frequent, the overall stress level of your marriage and life can be greatly reduced. Communication gives you a chance to work through issues rather than just hope they will suddenly go away.

What Did You Just Say?

During the first year of marriage, Leif and I often discovered that when we miscommunicated once, it became an escalating problem. One morning while we were on vacation, I asked Leif if he would go to the store to buy eggs for breakfast. He thought I asked him to make breakfast, so he prepared a bagel and cream cheese and brought it to me in bed. It was a kind act, and I didn't want to discourage him, so I smiled on the outside and offered a gracious "thank you." On the inside I was frustrated. I didn't want a bagel; I was craving scrambled eggs. After he delivered breakfast to my bedside, he turned on the television in the next room. While he was in the hall, I asked him, "What are you watching?" He looked at me, looked at the television, and walked away. In less than five minutes I had been transformed into a major grump. My husband had made me a breakfast I didn't care for and he obviously didn't want to spend time with me. When he came in the bedroom a few minutes later, I offered him a cold stare. "What's wrong?" he finally asked.

After unleashing my early morning fury, I learned the truth. Leif had misunderstood my desire for breakfast, and he had never heard my question while he was in the hall. A simple moment of miscommunication compounded itself. If we had not discussed it, the frustration would have continued to snowball throughout our day.

Such moments remind me that good communication is a work in progress. Even after a week of great talks and connecting points, you can still find yourself baffled by miscommunication. When those moments hit, it's important to stop and recount the events and patiently listen to the other side of the story.

SURPRISE NO. 14

The smallest miscommunication can lead to an epic fight.

Developing good communication takes time, skill, and intentional effort. More than likely you express yourself differently than your spouse. It's no wonder. You grew up in different families with different values and parenting models. Your spouse's family may be reserved, while yours is more expressive. Or vice versa. You may have a tendency to shut down, while your spouse uses talking as a method of processing information. The way you listen, discern, and respond to information can be wildly different. So when it comes to communicating, a small issue can become a big argument.

Shana, a 34-year-old who has been married seven years, says that if she and her husband are arguing, she estimates that 99 percent of the time it's because of miscommunication or because one of them has read into something or interpreted something the wrong way.

Jonathon, who has been married for 27 years, says he and his wife are the opposite of a lot of other couples. He talks a lot, even about feelings; his wife does not. "Early on, I would often ask, 'What's the matter?' She would just say, 'Nothing.' I finally learned to quit pestering her and focus my energies on creating an atmosphere that promotes conversation. She likes my time more than anything, so instead of coming home from work and trying to engage in a deep conversation, I learned to spend time with her and let her thoughts seep out gradually."

You or your spouse may be the better communicator in your relationship. If you are the stronger communicator, it's important to remember you can still improve. If you are not the strong communicator, you may be able to learn from your spouse. One young married woman noted that because her husband is the better communicator, he has helped draw out communication from her. "When we first met, I held everything inside and would withdraw for days or weeks," she says. "Now I can get things out much quicker and move on, keeping things from getting blown out of proportion and festering."

This is largely due to her husband creating a safe environment for her to share. "He wanted me to talk to him, and he would not give up until I did," she says. "After a while I saw that he cared and would listen; and we both grew from getting things out in the open and discussed. I thought too much damage would be done if I expressed my hurts and concerns; rather, it was far more damaging to keep them all in and to myself. Freedom and growth in our relationship took place as I began to be honest about my feelings, shared them, and then let them go."

In addition to creating a safe place to communicate, it can be helpful to practice some basic communication techniques.

Quick Tip: Talk with each other about what God is doing in your life.

Demand honesty. If you're going to truly communicate, create an atmosphere in which you and your spouse can honestly share what you're thinking, feeling, and desiring. You need to be able to express your likes and dislikes, hopes and dreams, hurts and disappointments. You need to be able to share yourself without judgment. Now, that doesn't give you or your spouse a permit to be hurtful. You both still need to choose your words wisely and pad them with the reminder that this is just what you're feeling. You also need to disclose everything you are feeling or thinking. Avoid the temptation to talk about three of the four issues that are on your mind during a sharing time. Mention all four. Leaving something out—even if it is small today—can have big effects on your relationship tomorrow.

> **Static-Free Communicating**
>
> What they said in your premarital counseling class was oh-so-true:
>
> - Avoid making accusatory or attacking statements toward your spouse.
> - Avoid making things personal if they could be perceived as harmful or hurtful.
> - Give the other person enough time to finish a story, make a point, or complete a thought.
> - Use relaxed body language.
> - Pray before responding.
> - Focus on sharing how an issue or event makes you feel.
> - Repeat back to the person what you think they said.
> - Always make eye contact.

Try to talk about things before they become an issue or have the opportunity to become emotionally charged. In a relationship, it is easy to swing to extremes. You may decide you need to point out every little fault, weakness, and problem or you may choose to suppress your feelings and responses to issues and shut down. Neither extreme is healthy.

Some actions—a shirt left on the floor, a bowl left in the sink, or a mispronounced word—are worth overlooking at times. They give us the opportunity to dismiss a small fault or oversight, to practice love and extend grace. But if you bite your tongue too many times, it's eventually going to unleash itself with a mighty fury.

Proverbs 29:11 reminds us that "A fool gives full vent to his anger, but a wise man keeps himself under control." If you have an issue with your spouse that's really getting on your nerves, then find a calm time to discuss it. Don't wait until a stressful moment to let the issue suddenly erupt in the middle of a conversation over an unrelated matter.

Tape record yourself. You may not be aware of how you come across when you communicate. At times I have an incredibly sharp tone in my voice that is both fierce and hurtful. It's not something I want to express or am even aware I'm expressing, but it happens nonetheless. One of the most helpful things Leif has done for me is to gently ask in those moments, "Did you mean to say it that way?" This gives me the opportunity to steady my response.

Mara, a-24-year-old newlywed who has been married for just over a year, says that she grew up in a family where they often communicated in a harsh and negative tone. "Now that I'm married, it has crossed over to my husband," she says. "It can come so naturally that I don't even realize I've hurt him. I have to constantly ask God for control over my tongue."

I recently spoke to one woman who said she had an intercom system in her house. It could be used to tape conversations in a room, and it became an incredibly valuable device in helping raise the awareness among family members of the tone they used in communication. Whether you hear yourself through a spouse, a friend, or a recording device, be sensitive to the tone you use.

Consider how your emotional, physical, and spiritual stamina are affecting your ability to communicate. Leslie, who has been married nearly three years, says she practices the S.H.A.L.T. principle. Conflict is most likely to arise when you are either Sick, Hungry, Angry, Lonely, or Tired. If you are aware of these in the other person or yourself, it goes a long way in avoiding a conflict. The hungry factor is particularly important if you or your spouse struggle with low blood sugar or diabetes.

Communicate your communication needs. That may seem a little redundant, but it's important to be sensitive to both your spouse's and your own communication needs. For example, whenever I call Leif at work, I always begin the conversation with the same phrase, "Is now a good time?" rather than launch into a three-minute discourse on whatever topic or issue I'd like to discuss. By doing so, Leif is given the opportunity to assess his situation. Does he have time to talk? Is he caught in a meeting? Will he be able to give me his full attention, or will he be wrestling with distractions? I know that by asking him a simple question—Is now a good time?—we are able to establish a foundation for healthy communication.

Learn how to listen. You or your spouse may be tops when it comes to talking and sharing vulnerably, but you also need to be an active listener. This means not thinking of your reply or what chicken recipe you want to use tonight when your spouse is talking. At crucial points in the dialogue, repeat back what your spouse just said. Sometimes what you heard isn't what your spouse meant. Everyone has certain filtering devices through which they take in information. So you may be hearing one message while your spouse is trying to communicate something entirely different.

A number of years ago I tried to compliment a woman I knew by saying, "You look really good. You've obviously worked hard and lost some weight." Rather than receive the compliment, she snapped back, "What are you trying to say? How big did I look to you before? How fat was I really?"

I didn't know what to say. I stammered an apology and learned two tough lessons. The first is to avoid commenting on anyone's size—even when it is meant to be an encouragement. The second lesson is that everyone interprets what they hear differently. Effective

Quick Tip: Encourage your spouse to pursue his or her dreams.

communication requires knowing what your partner is both hearing and saying.

In addition to being sensitive to your spouse's needs, you also need to be aware of your own. At times I just need to talk or vent. I don't want my husband to fix anything—though that's his natural tendency. I just want him to listen and allow me to process things out loud. We've actually developed a trigger term we use to let the other person know about our communication needs. One of us simply says, "I need to vent." From those four words on, we give each other full permission to say whatever needs to be said without a response, feedback, or judgment. The person is free to be fully honest and vulnerable, even if it's not pretty. This has been an invaluable tool for making it through difficult times.

> Psychologists agree that body language and tone of voice account for 93 percent of communication. Content comes in at a low 7 percent.
>
> (Taken from "Don't Say You're Sorry" by Chuck Lynch, *Marriage Partnership*, Fall 2003, Vol. 20, No. 3, p. 50.)

Be aware of your nonphysical communication. Do you realize that you communicate more with your body than with your mouth? You may say one thing verbally but communicate something completely different with your body. Be aware of your nonverbal communication, especially with your spouse. Look your spouse in the eye and avoid multitasking in order to show interest in what he or she is saying. Crossing your arms conveys a closed mind or defensiveness, while kicking back in a chair with your hands behind your head conveys a relaxed, vulnerable, friendly state of listening. Touching your spouse—through hand holding, sitting close together, or a casual embrace—can help your spouse know you're interested in listening and connecting with them.

Learn to hold your tongue. Sometimes good communication requires saying nothing at all. Justin, a newlywed who has been married less than a year and a half, says, "Sometimes the best thing

I can do is remain silent, literally biting my tongue to keep it from flapping away and causing more trouble." Justin notes that not responding sometimes frustrates his wife, but he explains that he just can't talk at the moment for one or more of the following reasons:

❋ If I talk there's a good chance I'll say something mean that will make things worse.

❋ Everything I say—regardless of how calm and nice I'm trying to be—will get turned against me to hurt me.

❋ I can get my feelings and emotions in check faster than my wife can.

With the last one, Justin has found that if he will sit down and gently pull his wife closer until she's sitting on his lap, then he can buy time for tensions to calm. "I hug and hold her for a bit in silence while I'm figuring out where I was wrong and then apologize for my wrong. If necessary I will share how what she said made me feel and how it hurt me. I am really careful at this point to make 'I' statements and not 'you' statements."

Learn to find a time of day just for the two of you. Maybe it's in the morning before work or after your spouse gets home. Maybe it's before bed or during a lunch hour. Carve out time that's just for you as a couple. Create a time when it's safe to freely discuss anything on your mind without distractions. Discuss your concerns, interests, current events, family, and future plans. Talk, share, and dream together.

Meg, a 20-year-old who has been married for a year and a half, says she and her husband try to go for a walk or a drive together every day. "We both know that, even if we have a hectic day or feel like we just aren't communicating in any form, we always have that time to reconnect," she says.

Quick Tip: Plan a romantic escapade.

Recognize that a transition period exists right after work when one or both of you will need to unwind. During the transition, you may need time on your own, or you may want to immediately recount the day's events with your spouse. Make sure you communicate your needs so you can be sensitive to each other.

Ask yourself how can you prevent miscommunication from happening again. Even if you become a world-class communicator, miscommunication will still happen. It is just part of being human. Communication patterns can develop that just don't work. Within a month or so of being married, Leif and I fell into the classic state of trying to talk to each other through walls. You know what I'm talking about. Leif was in the next room, and I assumed he could hear me. After all, I could hear myself, but all he could hear was a muffled request. The exchange bounced back and forth until one of us was willing to relocate so we could hear the person better. Sometimes little things—like an old answering machine, poor cell signal, or trying to talk through walls—can interfere with your communication. If you see an unhealthy pattern, make a change.

Questions for Reflection

1. How does communication affect your relationship with your spouse?

2. What can you do to become a better communicator?

3. Describe moments in your life when it's difficult to communicate. What are the common factors? How can you avoid them?

4. When was the last time you shared your hopes and dreams with your spouse?

Choose the Best Filing Status

Your marital status on December 31 determines whether you are considered married for that year. Married individuals may file their federal income tax return either jointly or separately in any given year. Choosing the right filing status may save you money.

- ☀ A joint return allows spouses to combine their income and to deduct combined deductions and expenses on a single tax return. Both spouses must sign the return and both are held responsible for the contents.

- ☀ With separate returns, each spouse signs, files, and is responsible for his or her own tax return. Each is taxed on his or her own income and can take only his or her individual deductions and credits. If one spouse itemizes deductions, the other must also.

Figuring the tax both ways can determine which filing status will result in the lowest tax. Usually, it's filing jointly. Publication 501, Exemptions, Standard Deduction, and Filing Information, has detailed information on filing status.

And Two Checkbooks Shall Become One?

eight

Love does not consist in gazing
at each other but in looking
outward in the same direction.

—ANTOINE DE SAINT-EXUPERY

MY HUSBAND IS NOT MUCH OF A DETAIL PERSON when it comes to numbers. I discovered this little truth when I asked him how much he weighed when he was born. "I think it was 16 or 18 pounds," he replied.

"What planet are you from?" I asked.

"Well, it was somewhere around there," he said confidently.

For Leif, numbers—outside of computers and engineering—are relative. Dozens and hundreds and millions tend to run together for him. In my husband's world, decimal points can be moved, traded, or erased without any consequence. As a result, he will quote some pretty funky statistics and dollar amounts. Then, when I least expect it, he'll be scarily accurate with a complex figure. This is all fine and well for dinner conversations and jokes, but when it comes to our finances, those extra zeros—or lack thereof—really make a difference.

Leif's attitude toward money is something I've never encountered before, and it has some real advantages. Year after year he goes to work, and he always seems to be amazed that they give him a paycheck every two weeks. He has never made the connection between work and money. He does what he loves. Money does not motivate him. Therefore, when he sees a person in need, his generosity is off the charts.

On the other extreme, I have been managing my parents' finances as well as my own for the last decade. I need to know what is in the checkbook to have a sense of security. Growing up with many seasons of feast and famine, the idea of having something to fall back on financially has become crucial. When we merged our finances and our ideas about money as a newlywed couple, we both had a lot of growing to do.

SURPRISE NO. 15

A little bit of money can cause a lot of conflicts.

Attitudes Toward Money

Generally, people tend to belong to one of two camps when it comes to money. You may be a blend of both, but more than likely, you'll lean toward spending or saving.

Saver or Spender
(Circle One)

Which would you use to describe yourself? Which would you use to describe your spouse? If you're a saver, then you'll both be looking for ways to cut costs, live efficiently, and make the wisest decisions with your money. You might be a saver if:

- ☼ You have a checking account, a savings account, and a retirement account.
- ☼ You have a 401K and/or stocks.

❈ You subscribe to *Consumer Reports*.

❈ You shop sales at the grocery store every week.

❈ You avoid excess charges on credit cards and ATMs like the plague.

❈ You actually know how to balance a checkbook.

You might be a spender if:

❈ You don't pay off your credit card bill each month.

❈ You are rarely caught shopping at a Wal-Mart.

❈ You have a natural disdain for coupons.

❈ You think the word "sale" is just one more reason to justify the purchase even if you don't really need it or can't really afford it.

❈ You need extra space for the clothes in your closet, most of which represent the latest fashions.

❈ You like what's hot, what's new, and what's cool, and when it comes to one particular area—whether it's technology, home furnishings, fashion, or your car—you don't want to own anything less than the best.

If you and your spouse are both savers, then you might be able to retire by age 40, but you won't have a lot of fun until then. If you and your spouse are both spenders, you're going to be able to enjoy being in style, but you are likely to end up in debt. If you married someone who is the opposite of you—whether it be a spender or saver—then you're going to have some natural conflict concerning how you respond to money, but you'll probably be better off in the long run. You'll get to go on great vacations and still have money when it's time to retire.

In most marriages, one person is the born saver and the other is the born spender, so you need to know what drives your spouse's attitudes toward money. Take time to ask yourself and your spouse the following questions:

> What does money mean to you?

> What does money buy for you?

Quick Tip: Slip a note into the book your spouse is reading.

Here are some possible answers:

Security	Acceptance
Self-worth	Love
Self-esteem	Accomplishment
Importance	Acclaim
Power	Friends
Freedom	Entertainment
Status	Happiness
Affirmation	Other

While money can buy all of the items listed above and more, you need to know how money motivates you. You may need money as a boost to your self-image or self-worth, while your spouse needs money to feel important and secure. Greed creeps into our lives when we want more money, but behind the desire is a force—whether a desire for approval, security, power, affirmation, or something else. Money can become an emotionally charged issue and point of conflict in a marriage.

God invites us to hold money with an open hand and trust Him to be the provider of things we really need. When we lay hold of money as if it is our own, it begins to take ownership of us. When we view money and possessions as items for which we are merely stewards and caretakers, then we begin to recognize money as something that empowers us to build God's kingdom rather than our own. Developing a healthy relationship with money takes time and often means having to learn the same hard lessons over and over again.

Merging Accounts

Trying to merge two people's finances can be a challenge. You may have multiple credit cards, checking accounts, saving accounts, retirement plans, and student loans. Plan on taking an afternoon to talk about your financial situation as a couple. Have an honest discussion about future goals and their financial implications. When do you want to buy a house? When do you want to have children? When do you want to retire? Do you plan to move, start a new hobby, or go back to school? How do you plan to save and invest for the future?

After you have spent some time talking about your individual financial situations, follow the simpler-is-better principle. What does that mean? Eliminate excess checking accounts, ATM cards, credit card accounts, and saving plans. When at all possible, streamline your finances into as few accounts as possible to make them easier and quicker to track.

A Few Financial Considerations

You may have talked to your spouse countless times about finances, but have you ever talked about the following?

- If one of you carries more debt or wealth into a marriage, how does that make the other person feel?

- If one of you decides to pursue further education, how will the debt affect your spouse?

- If one of your family members decides to give you a significant financial gift or one of you inherits a large amount of money, what will you do with the funds? Who will make the decision on how the money is spent?

This is also a good time to request a credit check for you and your spouse. Researching your credit rating can help you know what you need to do to be able to buy a car or house together and may uncover any fraudulent activities that have taken place through identity theft. Visit www.free creditreport.com for an initial free report.

After you slice and dice your excess credit cards and merge accounts, establish a system for handling your finances. What time of the month is the best for the two of you to pay bills? Who will be responsible for paying bills? Who will be responsible for ongoing financial demands, including sending in reimbursement requests to flex spending medical accounts, keeping an eye on investments, and balancing the checkbook? One of you is probably going to be more natural at handling finances. One person may volunteer for these responsibilities or you may decide to tackle them together. Even if one of you is handling the finances, update your partner on your financial situation regularly. You may want to invest in some financial management software such as Quicken or Home Tax Money Manager.

You also need to check out health, life, and auto insurance policies you have through your employer or carry on your own. Notify these companies that your marital status has changed. Regarding health insurance, you may need to add your spouse to the best, most affordable option and consider paying for an add-on that would cover pregnancy. On your life insurance, add your spouse as a beneficiary.

When it comes to finances, open communication will eliminate countless moments of friction and fights. So will a little organization. You and your spouse need to make time to develop a filing system for your receipts, taxes, checking statements, credit card bills, and other paperwork. You may find that a box or drawer with files or envelopes works best. You can develop any kind of system that works for you; just don't wait too long to start it.

Here's a quick tip: Near the area where you organize your finances, you may want to add a few extra files or envelopes for gift certificates, tax forms, frequent flyer and hotel programs, and coupon or discount cards.

SURPRISE NO. 16

When you get married, you have twice as many opportunities to give presents. Gift giving is one area of budgeting that usually catches newlyweds off guard. You buy gifts for your friends. Your spouse buys for his or her friends. That adds up to a lot of gifts. And after you've been showered with gifts from your own wedding, you may feel as though you need to repay others for their kindness. Plus, you have a whole new family to buy gifts for during the holidays. When you're establishing a budget, develop a general fixed amount for buying gifts.

Spending Limits

Some days the six-letter word "budget" feels like a four-letter word. It's a tough one to hear and an even harder one to live with. Though budgets remind me that my resources are not my own and the sky isn't the limit, they also enable Leif and me to live a more well-balanced and generous life.

If you haven't already done this, consider establishing a monthly budget for a two-month period. Use credit card receipts and checkbook statements to track spending for your fixed expenses, including rent, utilities, car payments, insurance, and food. If you have been paying for these items with cash or haven't gotten organized yet, then plan on spending the next two months tracking your expenditures. It may be helpful to collect receipts from every purchase and place them in an envelope. You may want to buy a small notebook to record expenditures. Experiment until you find a system that works for you, and consider using it beyond the first two months. When you know how much money you are spending and where it's going, then you're able to be on the offensive with your finances rather than on the defensive.

Spending limits can be a sore spot for newlyweds who previously had been able to spend their money exactly as they wanted without accountability. Suddenly, your money is not your own. Talk to your spouse about what your expectations and spending limits are. Provide a way for each person to enjoy the fruit of their labor—whether that means a new sweater at Banana Republic or a double Frappuccino at Starbucks. You can do this in a variety of ways.

The base number. Some couples establish a number—as small as $20 and as large as $100—that becomes the base number for a purchase. Anytime a potential purchase exceeds that number, they

Quick Tip: Embrace adventure. Go skydiving, camping, or parasailing together.

have to talk to their spouse first. This system promotes communication and eliminates surprises.

The allowance. Other couples work on an allowance system. Each spouse gets an allowable spending limit each week—beginning at $20 and growing larger—that he or she can use for discretionary spending, whether it's a CD, fly rod, or taking a friend to lunch.

The monthly meeting. A few couples I've spoken with have monthly meetings—usually at the beginning of the month—to review their finances. At that point they pay bills and calculate the extra money they can afford to spend during the month. Together they decide how much each individual can spend and if there are any items they want to buy together.

Remember to be flexible with your budgeting and money management. You're going to need to be ready and willing to revise your decisions on a regular basis.

Dangers of Debt

Debt and dieting have one thing in common: They both have advertisers who promise instant miracles that don't work. No matter how good the offer, no matter how low the APR, no matter how big the raise may be, living debt free comes down to one basic principle: You must live on less than what you make. That may sound silly because it's so simple, but it's also true.

Jim Paris, consumer advocate and author of *More for Your Money*, says that when it comes to balancing a budget, there are only two ways—you must either increase your income or cut expenses. "If someone says they can't do either one, then I say, 'I'll see you in bankruptcy court'," Paris says. "There are no other answers. You have to do it."

According to Paris, if a person only makes their minimum credit card payment, it will take an average of 25 years to pay off the debt, and the person will pay for the same item eight to ten times its original worth. That certainly makes you think before you purchase something you can't afford simply because it's on sale.

If you are in debt, then you need to obtain a lower-interest credit card. Transfer the balance to save money on interest, and put the extra money toward reducing the capital. If you are facing student loans, you may need to consider getting a part-time job or using any extra income to pay off the loan.

> The average man plans to spend $125.96 on Valentine's Day, whereas women, on the other hand, plan to spend $38.22.
>
> (TAKEN FROM: NRF 2003 VALENTINE'S DAY CONSUMER INTENTIONS AND ACTIONS SURVEY)

No matter what type of debt you are facing, if you and your spouse say, "I'm going to get out of debt," you will find a way. As a personal example, I told Leif he needed to be out of student loan debt before I would marry him. He ended up working massive amounts of overtime and moved back in with his parents in the months before the wedding, but it worked. The month before our ceremony, we were both able to celebrate being debt free.

The Ultimate Gift

One of the best ways to establish a healthy relationship with God is through tithing. By giving God the "first fruits" of what you earn, you are constantly reminded that He is the ultimate provider. If you or spouse did not grow up tithing—and giving 10 percent or whatever percentage you felt led to give back to God—begin taking that step of faith. If you feel you really can't afford it, then this is the perfect time to begin because it gives God the opportunity to prove His faithfulness in your lives.

Thinking About Going Back to School? Finding A Diploma-tic Solution

It's not uncommon for newlyweds to consider going to back to school to complete a degree or pursue another degree. Going back to school can put both an emotional and a financial strain on your relationship, so plan wisely.

Talk to your spouse realistically about how much time it is going to take, including time for classes, study, homework, finals, and commuting. You also need to calculate how many hours—if any—you can continue working while taking courses. Both you and your spouse need to realize schooling is going to cut into the time you can spend together, so discuss ways you can still build your relationship.

When it comes to funding your degree, you may want to consider finding an employer who offers tuition assistance. Some companies will allow employees to attend school part-time—sometimes in a related field—and foot the bill. Another option is the financial aid department of your college or university. They may have grants and scholarships available for your field of study. Check out the interest rates and all the strings attached to loans. Visit www.FinAid.com and www.gradview.com for additional information.

If you're attending graduate school and you're willing to teach an undergraduate course, your university may be willing to cover all or part of tuition and pay you a stipend. There's usually a lot of competition for these slots, but they're worth fighting for.

Finally, look for programs that will cover your tuition in return for service after graduation. Fields such as nursing and education often have programs that will pick up the tab for your degree if you're willing to take a job in a certain sector or location after graduation.

In the book of 2 Corinthians, Paul addresses the richness that comes with giving. He says,

> This most generous God who gives seed to the farmer that becomes bread for your meals is more than extravagant with you. He gives you something you can then give away, which grows into full-formed lives, robust in God, wealthy in every way, so that you can be generous in every way, producing with us great praise to God. Carrying out this social relief work involves far more than helping meet the bare needs of poor Christians. It also produces abundant and bountiful thanksgivings to God. This relief offering is a prod to live at your very best, showing your gratitude to God by being openly obedient to the plain meaning of the Message of Christ. You show your gratitude through your generous offerings to your needy brothers and sisters, and really toward everyone (2 Corinthians 9:10-13 MSG).

You not only meet other people's needs by giving faithfully, but also you motivate other people to action by your giving. When you give as a couple, you get to share with your spouse the rich increase that comes with generosity and experience the blessing together.

Emma, a 25-year-old who has been married for nine months, says that she was able to bring the tradition of tithing into her marriage. "It's been neat because we've both grown

Adding a Furry Friend

If you both were pet-less before you were married, you may eventually consider adding a pet to your life. Whether it's a cat, dog, iguana, or fish, you'll want to make sure your lifestyle will allow you to care for the animal. Also, add up the potential costs—which include food, veterinary bills, and pet sitters if you travel. If you can make it work, then consider getting a pet—even a furry friend—together. Dogs and cats tend to be able to sense when you're sick or having a rough day. When you're depressed, they still require you to care for them and require you to look outward to their needs instead of your own. And they're great for children, who learn about responsibility and unconditional love. They also teach children about death—a tough lesson, but one that is so necessary.

through it," she says. "It's amazing to tithe together and then see how God blesses us beyond anything we thought possible. You would never think that you can give that much away, and somehow we're still living comfortably."

Once you tithe, which is usually to a local church, you may be led to give additional funds away. The places you want to give money may not be the same for you and your spouse. Leif has a huge heart for children, so when it comes to giving money and time, he leans toward camps, youth events, and leaders who reach young people. I tend to be more mission-driven. Leif and I have had to compromise in where we send money in order to make it effective. Granted, we could send $10 or $20 to all of them, but we have had to prayerfully consider which ministries to support in order to write the checks we feel will make a difference.

Questions for Reflection

1. How do your attitudes toward spending or saving affect your spouse?

2. What do you need to do to have a more balanced, healthy attitude toward money?

3. What do you and your spouse need to do to get your finances in order?

4. Is there anything God is asking you to do with the money He has given you?

His Stuff, Her Stuff, and Too Much Stuff

nine

Simplicity is true bliss.

—AUTHOR UNKNOWN

LIKE MANY WOMEN, I HAVE A WEAKNESS for beauty products. When Leif and I shared our first bathroom, I thought it was cute that all his toiletries fit into a black travel bag. I figured he had to have more "product"—hair product, skin product, shaving product—tucked away in one of the boxes in storage. I tried to be self-sacrificing and give him the top drawer next to the sink, but by day three he still wasn't using it, so I figured it was fair game.

I waited for a moment when he was out to bring in my three large apple crate boxes marked "bathroom" in Sharpie magic marker. I began to unpack my arsenal of lotions, hair sprays, gels, shampoos, conditioners, mud masks, fingernail polish, cuticle clippers, feminine products, cold and stomach medication, and other miscellaneous beauty products. I filled the top drawer, second drawer, and the rest of the drawers. By the time I was finished, I had packed every square inch of the space under the sink and the precious eight inches that separated the sink from the toilet. I carried my three apple crate boxes to the garbage with a silly smirk on my face. I was satisfied.

Leif, on the other hand, was not.

"What's all this stuff?" he asked.

"It's product, honey!" I responded, grateful I had not married a metrosexual.

"Oh."

With that one-syllable reply, I knew my husband had been ushered into the wild, wacky world of living with a woman. I honestly thought I had won a major battle that day. I never suspected that the battle was just beginning, or that it was against a rather sly enemy: stuff.

SURPRISE NO. 17

If you thought one person could accumulate a lot of stuff,
just imagine how much self-storage space two people can fill.

Too much stuff. It's the American way. Everybody loves stuff. New stuff. Cool stuff. Techno stuff. Stuff is fun and hip and exciting—until it's overflowing from your closets, drawers, shelves, and every other hidden crevice in your home. When you get married, you can expect to double the amount of stuff you own. Two coffeepots. Three alarm clocks. Four and a half telephones—five, if only you could find the missing power adapter.

When Leif and I were living in the tiny apartment we nicknamed the Bat Cave, we didn't have a lot of space. So we did what every newlywed does: We put as much stuff as we could at his parents' house and the rest in self-storage. This tactic only delayed the inevitable; we were going to have to deal with all of our stuff.

One cold winter weekend, Leif and I began the difficult task of downsizing. Disposing of items from your past is not only emotionally draining, but also physically exhausting. If you're really sorting through your stuff, you're going to stumble upon small knick-knacks, gifts, cards, and photos that are going to transport you down memory lane. You may find a baseball that takes you back to little league, a letter jacket that transports you back to high school, a diploma that carries you back to college, or a stone that your best friend in third grade made you promise you'd keep forever.

If you need to go through this same process yourself, there are a few things to keep in mind.

You are not living on the ark. You don't need two of everything. It would be great to keep two coffeepots, two toasters, two vacuum cleaners, and two blenders just in case the other one breaks, but at some point you'll want to make a little bit more room in your home. If you have duplicates, ask yourself the following questions: Do I really need two of these? Which is the higher-quality product? Which is the newest? Which will be easier for my spouse or me to give away? And most importantly, who could benefit from the item we're going to give away? You may have a ministry or mission or nonprofit organization right down the road that needs what you're about to get rid of.

When it comes to style, you want to complement, not clash. Your stuff has its own style. Your spouse's style is probably a little different. As you sort through your boxes, you're going to find a variety of items that will qualify as home décor. You may really want to hold onto the purple vase you won as a door prize years ago. Your spouse may be infatuated with his framed motorcycle poster or tanned deer hide. But something has got to give if you're ever going to be able to call your house, apartment, or tepee a home.

If you haven't worn it in the last year, it's time to say goodbye. Leif and I are both guilty of holding onto clothes we don't wear. Some

Quick Tip: Find three new ways to express your love today.

of the pieces are tucked in the back of our closet and easy to over-look. Others are ones we hope to wear when we lose ten or more pounds—or at least that's what we keep telling ourselves.

We both have clothes in our closets that would get us arrested by the fashion police. We have given each other permission to go through each other's clothes and pull garments whose time has come. Occasionally we disagree and the shirt or pair of pants gets to come out for one last rendezvous, but for the most part the clothes go straight to Goodwill.

If you buy something new, make a pact to get rid of something old. Call me a woman, but I have a weakness for shoes. I love cool, trendy, comfy shoes. When they're on sale, they are irresistible. My husband and I have worked out an agreement: It's okay to buy them as long as I am willing to get rid of a pair I already own. It's a fair exchange. It makes me pause before picking out a new pair of san-dals, and it keeps my shoes fitting on one rather large rack. This basic principle—buy new and get rid of the old—should be prac-ticed with almost everything you purchase.

Remember that buying in bulk isn't always better. I love Costco. I think it's one of the coolest stores on the planet. They have incred-ible meat, delicious cheeses, black olives, books, computers, and everything you could ever need—supersized. I think I could live a very happy life inside a Costco.

While warehouse stores are great for buying products such as spaghetti sauce, dishwashing detergent, and toilet paper, I'm still struggling to make a dent in the pound of parsley flakes, gallon of shampoo, and giant jar of aspirin I bought two years ago. Now, if we had six kids running around, I would be able to use all those products in bulk, but with just the two of us it's a little much.

Getting rid of stuff gives you the opportunity to learn to share. If you go into marriage with the attitude *what's mine is mine and what's yours we'll share*, you are going to have a pretty bumpy road ahead of you.

Cutting down on the amount of stuff you have gives you the opportunity to share with your spouse and grow as an individual. When you're resistant to part with a particular item, ask yourself why it's so important to you. What value does it have to you? Is it memorabilia? Is it something you don't want to share? One newlywed woman admitted she didn't want to share her guitar with her husband. She wanted to keep it for herself. After some time and prayer, she was willing to let her husband get rid of his guitar and use hers.

Everyone should be allowed to keep at least one box. You can cut back, downsize, and develop a Pottery Barn look in your home, but you still need to have a place where each of you gets to keep some special treasures. Maybe it's a box, a chest, or a set of drawers. Maybe it's a corner of the attic. After you get rid of the excess, establish a place where you and your spouse can store lifelong treasures—photos, jewelry, dried flowers, foreign coins—all those little mementos that make life rich.

Questions for Reflection

1. Do you have any possessions that tend to possess you? If so, describe them. Why do they mean so much to you?

2. Do you have any boxes you haven't opened in more than a year? If so, consider sorting through them and giving items away.

3. Between you and your spouse, which items are you willing to carry around for the next 20 years?

4. What can you do to avoid collecting even more stuff in the future?

5. Have you shared the stories behind the items you are keeping with your spouse?

The Games We Play

In order to encourage each other and have some fun, Leif and I play the Points Game, which I learned from my parents. Each of us is given a "point" every time we do something right, respond to someone as Jesus would, or make a small prediction on something that comes true. We simply say "Point for Margaret" or "Point for Leif" and write an imaginary point in the air with our index finger to acknowledge the other person. Like the show *Whose Line Is It Anyway?* we don't keep track of the points, but we do give bonus points for extra acts of kindness or guessing the outcome of events correctly. It puts us in the habit of seeing the best in each other and prevents us from echoing the dreaded words, "I told you so."

ten | Eating for Two— The Health and Nutrition of Married Life

Good health and good sense are two of life's greatest blessings.

—PUBLIUS SYRUS

IT HAS BEEN SAID THAT THE WAY TO A MAN'S HEART IS through his stomach. If that's true, then we're all in big trouble—especially during the first few years of marriage.

Most young couples experience weight gain when they get married. Food can often become a love language between two spouses. To express love, couples cook for each other, eat out together, and surprise each other with treats. As a single, you probably had a number of meals you skipped simply because you weren't hungry. If you're married—and there's dinner on the table—you will end up eating something even if you're not hungry. While enjoying the newlywed phase of your marriage, you may find yourself in a time crunch to work out. Add up all these factors, and you're going to discover some unwanted pounds.

As a wife, you may think you have to cook a full meal every night—complete with vegetable, protein, and starch. In addition, you may find that socializing with other couples includes a meal. When was the last time you went to a church event that didn't include food?

SURPRISE NO. 18

If you're not careful, you can put on a lot of weight during your first year of marriage.

The meal time has been a sacred time for thousands of years. Think of the Last Supper or when Jesus appeared on the beach after His resurrection in John 21. The disciples were out fishing, and when they came to shore, breakfast was ready. Meals provide time to connect; eating is an activity that brings souls together.

Now that you're married, you'll be tempted with new treats your spouse will bring home. When Leif and I were first married, he would purchase bags of chips and boxes of cookies and put them on a top shelf assuming I would have the willpower to resist these tempting treats. It only took a few days for him to figure out he was wrong. My willpower when it comes to junk food only extends to not buying and bringing it into the house. Once it's in my kitchen cabinet, it's fair game.

We have been able to work out a compromise. Leif doesn't bring junk food into the house. He enjoys it at barbecues, picnics, and the restaurants we enjoy. If he needs a bag of chips, he is welcome to have them as long as I don't know where they are. It's a unique agreement that works for us.

It's never too early to start developing a healthy lifestyle as a couple. Here are a few things to keep in mind.

Keep an eye on the scales. Weight can creep on as a newlywed. It's important to keep an eye on what you may be gaining. If you're not fond of stepping on a scale, then have a pair of pants or a shirt you can try on. If you can't fit into your favorite piece of clothing, then it's probably time to skip appetizers and dessert. If your spouse is gracious, you can eat yourself into an unhealthy size without even knowing it. Davie, a 22-year-old who has been married for 15 months, estimates he put on close to 40 pounds during the first year of marriage. He and his wife have begun exercising more regularly and passing on dessert. Together, they're starting to lose weight.

Spend more on groceries. This can be a tough one, especially if you have a tight budget. Unfortunately, healthy food is generally more expensive. Corn-based products—including chips and foods with corn syrup—tend to be less expensive because corn is subsidized by the U.S. government. Fresh vegetables, fruits, and lean cuts of meat are almost always more expensive, but they're worth it. Not only do they help to keep you lean and provide valuable vitamins and nutrients, but these types of food will help you stay healthy for years to come.

Remember that eating out is meant to be special. Eating out isn't just tough on your pocketbook, it's also hard on your waistline. When you eat out, you don't get to choose the ingredients or portions. Restaurants provide an atmosphere that promotes overeating and consuming an entire day's worth of calories in a single meal. Studies show that cooking at home can save you as much as 1000 calories per meal. As fun as eating out can be, remember to eat at home on a regular basis for a healthier lifestyle.

Establish activities with couples and friends that don't include food. Go for a hike. Play basketball. Go to the beach. Begin developing friendships and activities that aren't centered on food. You will appreciate all of the effort later.

Become workout partners. This can be a touchy issue for young couples, but it's important to encourage each other to exercise. You

Quick Tip: Sing a song of love to your spouse—even if you can't sing.

may go to the gym at the same time, or you may go for a walk or run while your spouse takes a bike ride. Whatever system works for you, make sure you're encouraging your spouse to exercise and giving the person the actual time to do it.

> **Four Things to Trim from Your Diet**
>
> 1. Sugar
> 2. Refined grains (white flour)
> 3. High-processed snack foods
> 4. Soda

Don't try to become your spouse's motivation. Few things can kill a healthy relationship faster than someone forcing you to become healthy. You can challenge and encourage your spouse to lose weight and exercise more, but this should be done tenderly and graciously. Positive reinforcement is far more powerful than criticism. If you say too much about your spouse's size, frame, or weight, your spouse will have a hard time believing you actually accept them for who they are, and you'll be seen as a nag.

Plan on eating healthy. Almost everyone wants to eat healthier, but think about what you need to do to eat more nutritiously. Maybe that means eating a salad before you go to a dinner party to avoid overeating if you are super hungry. Or you may want to develop a mental list of healthier restaurants in your area so that, when someone asks you where you want to go to eat, you have a place in mind that won't bust your waistline.

Invest in healthy cookbooks. Depending on where you and your spouse were raised, you probably have different ideas about cooking and nutrition. Buy a subscription to *Cooking Light*. Invest in some new low-fat or low-carb cookbooks. Develop new techniques of making favorite recipes a little healthier.

Change your lifestyle together. Everyone wants to avoid the four-letter word "diet" whenever possible. Most nutritionists agree that is a good idea because weight loss comes primarily from a change of lifestyle rather than a diet, which can put you on a roller coaster

Quick Tip: Give a gift for no reason.

of weight loss and gaining the weight back. Whatever food lifestyle you choose—limited fat or carbs, organic, vegan, or smaller portions—try to get your partner on board. This will eliminate having to prepare two meals at dinnertime as well as put you on the same course for weight loss. Keep realistic expectations about losing weight. Remember that men have a larger amount of muscle mass than women. Your spouse probably isn't going to lose weight at the same rate you do.

Go for walks. Walking is an incredible form of exercise that is often overlooked. A long walk with your spouse will not only burn calories but also provide a time for you to connect and strengthen your relationship. Instead of watching *Fear Factor* after dinner, go for a stroll.

Whatever it takes, keep yourself physically in shape. Get in a pattern of exercising together, and remember that setting proper eating habits early in a marriage will add health and years to both your lives.

Questions for Reflection

1. How have your eating patterns changed since you were married? How have they improved?

2. How can you and your spouse encourage each other in pursuing a healthy lifestyle?

3. In what areas do you encourage each other to have a less-than-healthy lifestyle?

4. What lifestyle changes can you and your spouse make in order to eat better and exercise more this month?

Four Ways to Jump-start Romance

one Give your bedroom a makeover. You don't have to drop big bucks to freshen up your bedroom. Just a little bit of money and some time can make a big difference. Begin by cleaning the room. Dust, wipe down mirrors, and vacuum. Clear out any clutter. Wash your bedding with some sweet-smelling fabric softener. Buy some candles from a local retailer and put them in small groups of two to four around the room, being sensitive to any potential fire hazards. While you're shopping, pick up a few fresh roses and drop petals across the bedspread and surrounding floor. Select some fine chocolates or mints and place them on both pillows.

two It's time to shine the candlesticks. There's nothing like a romantic meal to capture your spouse's heart. If you don't have all day to cook, then consider having food delivered 15 minutes before your spouse gets home. Prepare the dining room table with a fresh tablecloth, cloth napkins, and your finest silverware and plates. Depending on the lighting in the room, you may want to consider buying some lower wattage light bulbs to create a serene setting. When your spouse comes home, simply greet with a kiss and begin enjoying the evening together.

three Book a surprise getaway. If you and your spouse have a busy schedule, the surprise in the getaway may not be which weekend you go, but rather where you go. Search websites such as www.priceline.com and www.hotwire.com for affordable four- and five-star hotels in surrounding cities. As long as it's just the two of you, it will be a memorable and enjoyable getaway.

four Speak the language of love. Your spouse has a unique love language—maybe it's quality time, acts of service, gifts, verbal affirmation, or touch. If you haven't already, then you and your spouse should consider reading Dr. Gary Chapman's *The Five Love Languages*. Once you identify your spouse's love language, shower the one you married with the time, service, gifts, affirmation, or touch your spouse naturally desires.

eleven

Birds, Bees, and What No One Told Me About Sex

A fulfilling sex life colors the marriage from top to bottom and is a powerful marital glue—even stronger than children, common values, faith or dreams.

—KEVIN LEMAN

SHORTLY AFTER WE WERE MARRIED, I WAS HELPING take care of my aunt's bed-and-breakfast in Alaska when a rather interesting guest spent a few nights at the inn. During one of our morning conversations— between bites of freshly baked scones—she told me about an amazing village she had visited earlier that year called Point Hope. Located above the Arctic Circle on a plain, the native people didn't have any access to wood to build their homes, so instead they dug holes in the ground and used whalebones to build their roofs. She explained that if you visit Point Hope today, you can still see some of these structures.

I was hooked. More than anything I wanted to go to Point Hope. When the holidays rolled around and my husband asked me what I wanted for Christmas, I told him about the remarkable town built with whale bones. He gave in to my wild request—after all, it was our first Christmas as a couple—and I began to plan the trip. I quickly learned that getting to Point Hope was no easy matter, and we'd have to pick a nearby town as a base for a charter flight into the village. We decided to wait until May—when there were plenty of hours of daylight and above-freezing temperatures—to make the trip. We would stay in Kotzebue, Alaska, for three nights at a bed-and-breakfast and schedule a day trip into Point Hope. I made the reservations and spent the next five months daydreaming and romanticizing about the trip.

That was my first mistake.

My second mistake was booking a bed-and-breakfast off the Internet, which only showed one photo of the premises—the sign outside. Let's just say that the peeling paint and the funky-smelling room were not what I had envisioned. Along the way, the airline lost my luggage, but everything was still okay, because I was going to get to see whalebone houses.

We rose early in the morning to catch our flight to Point Hope. I opened the refrigerator and found our breakfast—yogurt, bagels, and various baked goods—waiting to be eaten. The only problem was that they had been waiting a long time; all the dates on the food items were more than a month past due. No problem. I was still going to see my whalebones.

We arrived at the airport a little hungry and discovered the flight was delayed for more than an hour. We caught up on the latest issues of *People* and *National Enquirer* that were sitting around in the charter airline's lobby and finally got on board the 19-seat passenger plane for the hour-long flight. Because there wasn't a wall between the

Quick Tip: Have a pillow fight.

cockpit and passenger area, I enjoyed watching all of the gauges that showed our altitude and speed.

I began to get a little concerned though, when we descended to 500 feet and still couldn't see the ground due to fog. The altimeter continued to drop to 300, 200, 100 feet, and outside the window was still solid fog. I looked at my husband and asked if we were going to be okay. He offered a confident nod that everything was going to be fine. (I discovered later that he was lying.) After leveling at 15 feet off the ground, we still couldn't see it, and a buzzing alarm in the cockpit was heard throughout the aircraft repeating "Minimum, minimum." I looked out the window. I couldn't see the ground. I knew we were going to crash.

At that moment, I prayed the most honest prayer I had prayed in a long time. *God, please help us, but if You don't save us, then please forgive me for all of my sins and the ways I've shortchanged You. Thank You for my family, for giving me an incredible husband, and for letting me have sex. I love You. Amen.*

I braced for the crash.

At that moment the captain reached over and grabbed the controls from the copilot, and we began a steep ascent banking to the left. Everyone on the plane was quiet until we realized we were all still alive. A few people were crying. Some were laughing. Others were in a dazed state. Then the pilot announced we were going back for a second attempt at landing. I white-knuckled the armrests and prepared for another face-off with death.

In less than five minutes we were on the ground. When we stepped off the plane, we learned what had happened: the pilot had miscalculated the landing field and missed the airstrip. We were on the right side of the runway—the side with all the towers, wires, and poles. If we had clipped any one of them during the climb out, we would have crashed.

We also learned that we were the first flight to get into Point Hope in three days due to the weather, so if we didn't get back on the plane, there was no telling how long we would be staying in this remote village. I could see the whalebone structures in the foggy distance from the airfield—a half mile or so away—but the only flight that could guarantee that we'd get to leave that day was leaving in ten minutes. I made one last effort to see those old, dried bones and ran into the fields, but there was no way I was going to make it in time. I returned to the small aircraft, took my seat, and cried my way back to that oh-so-disappointing bed-and-breakfast in Kotzebue, where I less-than-successfully tried to put on a happy face for the remainder of the weekend.

I learned valuable lessons from that trip. First, don't plan romantic getaways above the Arctic Circle, and if you do, bring your own 300-thread-count sheets. Second, faced with the possibility of dying, your prayers get really honest and vulnerable. And in that moment I had thanked God for sex.

Starting from Scratch

Because Leif and I decided to wait until we were married to have sex (and by God's grace and some incredible parenting, we made it), I think that just about everything about sex could be described as a surprise.

Being a journalist at heart, I wasn't going into my wedding night without doing some solid research. I picked up some helpful Christian books, including Kevin Leman's *Sheet Music*, and I made a mental list of female friends with whom I'd be comfortable discussing the "s" word. The sad fact is that sex isn't a word you can say around just anyone, especially many Christians. Some people aren't comfortable with it—even if they have been doing it for years—and they have a magical way of making you feel even more uncomfortable about it if you dare to raise the subject.

I steered away from anyone who couldn't actually say the "s" word and picked up the phone to call the four people on the planet

Quick Tip: Flirt with your spouse at least once a day.

I could openly ask questions about this great, mysterious activity that was going to happen after we said "I do." I didn't find out much, but I found out enough: Sex is messy, fun, and painful on your first night. I was still a little fuzzy about how things really went together or really worked, but I knew enough, after talking to my girlfriends, to know that things were going to be okay...eventually.

I don't know if my wedding night was typical or not. In fact, I don't really know what is typical because most women describe the big night in one of three ways: "It was wonderful." "It hurt." "It gets better." Somehow—in one night—I managed to qualify for all three.

Though we were married at 11 A.M., the party didn't end until 12 hours later. That evening, for the first time, as we were preparing to bathe, we saw each other naked. It was a strange yet freeing feeling to know and to be known so intimately by someone else. We had agreed beforehand that we weren't going to have sex on our wedding night. I had heard enough horror stories of women who just wanted to talk about the day's events and instead got jumped by their overly eager husbands that I wanted to remove any pressure. That lasted about 20 minutes. Then, I jumped him.

Poor guy. I don't think he knew what hit him, and I don't think he knew what hit me. It was over before either of us knew what happened. I remember thinking, *Did we just have sex?* Neither of us really knew. Over the next few weeks and months, I figured it out. And, yes, we did have the "s" word on our wedding night.

> In a recent survey, 37,000 people were asked: "How many times per month do you have sex?"
>
> 1-5: 37%
>
> 6-10: 23%
>
> 11-15:12%
>
> More than 15: 10%
>
> (THE LOVE SURVEY, *O MAGAZINE*, FEBRUARY 2004, P. 33.)

Figuring Stuff Out

Even after a year of regular practice, I'm still a novice at this "s" thing. I am convinced that sex is a lot like learning to bowl. It takes a lot of practice to get really good at it. Some days you'll get lucky and play an incredible game, and other days your ball just rolls in the gutter. The good thing about sex, though, is that no one has to keep score.

During the first month of our marriage, I learned that sex doesn't look anything like what I had seen in the movies. In the movies, lovers lie for hours holding each other in a warm, romantic embrace after sex. In reality, I have to get up to use the bathroom immediately or else I risk getting a urinary tract infection. In the movies, lovers wake up and have sex and passionate kisses in the morning. In reality, we're both at the sink with Colgate or we avoid the lip-locking altogether. In the movies, the lovemaking goes on for what seems like forever. In reality, we have jobs, responsibilities, and demands that require us to fall asleep by a certain time. Hollywood doesn't look like the real world and that's okay, because there are some things that the silver screen just can't capture. Like the sense of connectedness that comes from making love. Or the warm smile on his face, or the soft glow on yours. Hollywood can't convey the reality that sex is so much more than an orgasm and can be a form of worship—glorifying God—when done between a married couple.

SURPRISE NO. 19

The secret to really hot sex is to have it often with your spouse.

One of the biggest surprises for me about sex is how many things get in the way of actually doing it. If two married people want to have sex, they should be able to do it at any time, but the demands of life easily interfere. I recently made a list of things that prevent my husband and me from getting together and getting it on. Can you relate to any of these?

Stress/Anxiety	Exhaustion
Busyness	Traveling apart from each other
Children	Pressure to perform sexually
Unresolved conflict	Lack of emotional connectedness
Menstrual cycle	Illness or sickness
Not enough time	Poor physical condition
Resentment	Other _____

With so many things standing between my husband and me having sex, I realize that I need to take a more proactive role in making it happen. Some days it means saying no to offers from friends to get together so that we can have time to connect emotionally and physically. Other times it means being willing to have sex even when one of us doesn't particularly feel like it.

Communication is essential when it comes to sex, but it certainly isn't easy. Early in our marriage Leif and I formed a pattern of talking about sex right after we were done. During this debriefing (pardon the pun), we talked about what we liked and disliked, when we climaxed, and what we enjoyed most about the experience. By being honest with each other and talking candidly about our experiences, our intimate times are continuing to improve and become even more enjoyable.

The Ghosts of Relationships Past

While my husband and I were blessed to head into marriage as virgins, many of my friends succumbed to sexual temptation before making it to the altar.

Even with mistakes in your background, sex within marriage can still be marvelous, but it can come with some additional challenges—like the ghosts of relationships past.

Quick Tip: Remember that it's more important to be righteous than right.

One of my close friends has been married for almost a decade for the second time, and she admits that while this marriage has been a wonderful, healing experience, sometimes old thoughts, memories, and impressions try to rear their ugly heads in the bedroom.

"I understand so much better now why I was supposed to wait," she says. "The New Testament talks about sexual sin as being the sin that you do to your own body—against your own self—and that is so true. It can be horrifying when, in the midst of passion, a fleeting memory of intimacy with someone of the past tries to creep in. Or when you deal with the guilty feeling that comes with remembering past relationships that were destructive emotionally, but actually better sexually. You certainly don't want to compare, but you can't help it. With a clean slate, there's nothing to judge against. You get to learn it all—and be good or bad in bed—with only each other."

My friend says that the Scripture verses that speak of taking control of your thoughts and taking authority over them still help her in situations where her mind tries to go down memory lane. Still, she says that starting marriage as virgins definitely has advantages, even beyond the fact that that is the way God planned it.

"I know I am forgiven, but that doesn't mean my mind has automatically forgotten," she says. "Also, I had developed some bad habits in order to be 'pleasing' to my former spouse. Sometimes I faked my climaxes just to get finished with sex and make him think he was wonderful. In my new marriage, sex was sometimes frustrating because I was used to being deceptive. This time I wanted to be honest, but it made me very insecure because I felt like it took me such a long time and I wasn't affirming him enough by being instantly 'responsive.'"

If you had sex with other partners, or even with your own spouse before marriage, guilt over the past can also be a barrier to having good sex. So can miscommunication and regret that these are not first-time discoveries for you as a couple. If a former partner was loud or talkative in bed, and your new spouse is very quiet, you may feel that you are not pleasing your mate. In my friend's case, even though she knows God's forgiveness was instant and total, the damage caused by sinning against her own flesh did not disappear overnight. It took years of unconditional love, reassurances, and prayer with her spouse to completely shed old, bad habits and insecurities to be able to fully enjoy sex each and every time.

Tips for Overcoming the Past

1. Ask God and your spouse for forgiveness.

2. Accept their forgiveness. This is crucial! Don't let the enemy keep dredging up your past mistakes.

3. Work on communicating openly with your spouse without bringing up too many details of the past.

4. Never fake your orgasms.

5. Pray about your sex life together.

6. Find ways of trying something new and exciting together.

The moment an unwanted thought or insecurity tries to make its way in, take it captive. The Bible says you have the power to do that. Believe it!

Questions for Reflection

1. What surprised you about sex with your spouse?

2. How has sex with your spouse improved since you got married?

3. What could you and your spouse do to increase your level of communication about sex?

For Him Only— Being the Best Spouse You Can Be

twelve

Note:
I asked my
husband, Leif, to
write this chapter.

*Love does not demand
its own way.*

—I Corinthians 13:5 NLT

EVERY HUSBAND AND EVERY WIFE ARE DIFFERENT.

Our strengths and weakness, though similar, are different. What my wife might swoon over—yours might respond to with "What was he thinking?" Whatever you choose to do for your wife, make sure it's something she would like. The more you get to know her, the better off you'll both be.

I was one of those clueless guys in junior high who decided I was mature enough—at 12 or 13—to pick all the characteristics of the wife I was going to have. And I thought the girl I chose would instantly know I was the one for her. I could go into a long story at this point involving a pastor's daughter, summer camp, and a headless teddy bear, but I think you get the picture. Needless to say, I really didn't know nearly as much as I thought I did. And I certainly did not know her as well as I thought I did. This leads me to the first piece of the puzzle that forms a godly husband: Get to know the girl, lady, and woman who is your wife.

Get to Know Your Wife

At the beginning of marriage, you may think you've got your wife pretty well figured out, but getting her to the altar and keeping her smiling for 20 years or more are two very different things. You've probably already discovered her favorite restaurant, flower, and food. (Margaret's are Ludvig's Bistro in Sitka, daisies, and chocolate.) Still, those preferences are things you can learn in junior high romances. I think I can do better than that. I think you can too.

I approach getting to know Margaret as though I am Tom Cruise in *Mission Impossible*. Of course, I'm probably closer to being a spy in a made-for-TV film on *Lifetime,* but that's beside the point. I've crossed over from the way-too-easy "What was that flower you liked?" into being a little more sophisticated.

This is where you can get creative and have fun. I try to get some ideas from my wife's friends.

If Margaret is talking to a long-time friend on the phone, I will innocently ask if I can say hello. The people she spent a lot of time with before she met me are a veritable cornucopia of good information. Whether the person is a parent, sorority sister, or former coworker, I have been able to glean some pretty interesting historical data from them. Sometimes I'm pretty bold and just ask what they think she would like as a gift or surprise, and other times I have to maneuver around the typical questions to get to something useful. One word of warning—beware of getting too close to any of your wife's friends.

I've Researched My Wife. Now What Do I Do?

All the good tips you've snagged from friends and family are great, but you have to use them or you have just wasted a bunch of time.

FOR HIM ONLY

Can I let you in on a secret? I'm a full-blown romantic. I love buying flowers for my wife. I actually like watching *Sleepless in Seattle* and *You've Got Mail*. I like the idea of sweeping Margaret off her feet. Originally I tried to do this by giving gifts. I gave my wife a number of what I thought were very creative gifts that really bombed. (For instance, don't buy your wife sporting equipment unless you *know* she wants it.) Every so often, however, I pick a winner, and that makes it worth all the effort.

As I have gotten to know Margaret on a deeper lever, I have discovered that more than spending money on gifts, she wants my time and attention. She really wants that more than anything else. I know that showing up unexpectedly to go to a movie or asking her to go on a long walk are tops on her list, but I'm always looking for more ideas.

Opening any door for her makes my heart sing, and when we travel I love being able to carry all the bags. I guess what I get the biggest kick out of is just serving her. The best example of service I have experienced with Margaret so far was at a conference called Elevate put on by the North American Mission Board of the Southern Baptist Convention in Charlotte, North Carolina. She had been asked to speak at the conference, and I had saved up enough vacation time and frequent flier miles to attend the event with her. I got to introduce myself as her personal assistant, though when I was initially registered as Mr. Feinberg (my wife's maiden name) I was a little annoyed. Then I saw the twinkle in the registration lady's eye. She was pulling a prank. Before we left on the trip, I had decided I was going to make myself responsible to make sure Margaret got to where she needed to go, had books to pass out, and whatever else she needed.

Those three days were so much fun!

She would ask me for a pen, paper, business card, or some other little detail; and I would pull it from my backpack without

Quick Tip: If your spouse gets really mad, stay kind and gentle.

blinking an eye. I don't know what kind of relationship you have with your wife or if you have any similar opportunities to serve her in what she does, but if you do I can pretty much guarantee it will be a worthwhile experience for you—even if it means changing dirty diapers. If you look at your married friends, you'll find that husbands with contented wives are men who take time to look around to see what they can do to serve their wives and then do it.

When I was ten, I remember making a conscious decision to watch all of the successful marriages that I was around and try to learn from them. I was blessed to be the oldest son in a family where both of my parents are still married and live together and still actively demonstrate their love for each other. In addition, I was also brought up in a church where the majority of the congregation was pretty healthy relationally—whether single or married with kids or grand-kids.

Some amazing couples who informally adopted me after I left Sitka—the Stampers in Arizona, the Gerlachs in Colorado, and the Younies in Texas—extremely blessed me as I lived with them and watched them interact with each other. One of the things I picked up on from observing these folks is the importance of doing things together that you both enjoy.

Whether it was serving at a church together, watching movies they both liked, or doing chores around the house, the couples with successful marriages showed me that finding activities to do together is really important.

The Younies had this gorgeous backyard with lots of trees, grass, and a garden. Every weekend Doug and Kate would get up, have breakfast together, and then go work out in the yard. They didn't have to be joined at the hip. Mostly Doug would grab the lawn mower and Kate would be weeding in the garden. But when it came to planning, they would sit in the shade with cool drinks and dream

Quick Tip: Play hooky from work one day and enjoy each other.

FOR HIM ONLY

together about what they wanted their yard to look like in the future. Even though the contributions they made to the yard were done individually, the end result always brought pleasure to both. Kate enjoyed watching their puppy romp in the freshly cut grass, and Doug liked serving homegrown vegetables with his barbecued masterpieces.

SURPRISE NO. 20

Good, old-fashioned fun is a powerful force
in a relationship.

Margaret and I don't own a home where we can work in a backyard yet, but we are slowly figuring out some things that we enjoy doing together. It gets complicated since Margaret likes the outdoors and I'm an indoor kind of guy, but we are making it work. I'm slowly discovering the real joys of taking walks together after I get off of work. Now, on nice days, I'm even skipping lunch and going for a quick stroll with Margaret to catch up and connect. At the same time, we are beginning to cook together in the kitchen and have a blast while doing it.

I'm thankful that we are discovering more and more activities we enjoy doing together. I love to read, but Margaret is opening my eyes to all of the adventures that wait outside the pages of a book. We have tried some activities that we wouldn't repeat, but I can tell you that for every idea we try that fails, we have found another that is worth doing again. Plus, it gives us plenty of laughs.

Serving God Together

One of the main things that brought Margaret and me together is our love for Christ. Our beliefs are similar, but how we choose to serve God are two very different things. I love going to church. Every night of the week would work just fine for me. Margaret prefers a once-a-week service, plus a small-group meeting.

This has led to a compromise on both of our parts. I helped start a more contemporary, outreach-centered service at the church on Saturday nights, and Margaret loves that service. I've given up going to church on Sunday mornings, and we use the time to worship in our home together. Neither of us gets exactly what we want, but I've discovered that our times of worship on Sunday morning are infinitely richer and more varied than what I have ever experienced in the past.

More than just worshiping together, we have started to work together on various projects. Over the last year we have led a junior high Sunday school class that has opened both of our eyes to different experiences. The lessons learned from introducing Jesus to a younger generation has been a real treat and also challenged both of us to become better communicators.

As our lives continue to intertwine and our callings mesh together, I imagine that God will lead us through many different opportunities to serve Him. I am really looking forward to doing many of those things with my wife.

Tell Her the Truth

One thing that has changed since my wife and I were married is that I have learned that I need to tell her the whole truth all the time. When we were dating, I constantly tried to keep her from learning anything negative about me. She knew I didn't understand money or have lots of close friends, but character flaws were kept hidden. The extent of my self-centeredness was under wraps until a couple months into our marriage. We both knew we were imperfect going into it, but I think we actually thought we could be on our best behavior for the rest of our lives. Needless to say, we were wrong.

I discovered that I couldn't go out and spend an extra $50 or $100 on some random whim, because sooner or later we would balance the checkbook and then I'd have to scramble to explain the missing funds. She was able to see through my excuse that "It was for those flowers I bought you—don't you remember?" (Actual cost—$18 for flowers and $32 for candy, chips, and soda.) When she exposed my lies, I could see the hurt on her face; and it was something I never want to see again. I've decided I will tell her everything whenever she asks. This honesty in our marriage has rebuilt the trust that my omissions and deception initially tore down. Now I think she knows that when she asks I'll tell her the truth, even when it makes me look bad.

One real positive twist to this has been that when she asks me what I'm thinking about, I can actually just spit out whatever I'm thinking. Whether it's "I wish we weren't walking in the sun right now" or "Literally, nothing," she knows I'm not hiding something from her.

It's All About Her

In the Bible our relationships with our wives are compared to the relationship between Christ and the church. It's a relationship built on self-sacrifice. As men we are called to be the spiritual leaders of the family, and that isn't always easy. It may mean sacrificing the latest Tom Clancy novel to study the Bible or skipping the latest sports game to make time to pray. But our wives need to know we're studying the Scripture and praying for them.

Honoring our wives is biblical as well. I had to restrain myself from verbally assaulting someone who asked how my "old lady" was doing. Maybe this is common for you or you don't think this is a big deal, but I think my wife is beautiful, and when most people use this phrase it isn't meant in a positive way. I will not have anyone talk about my wife without showing her respect. If I hold other people accountable, I need to be responsible in this area myself. If you ask my wife, she'll tell you I rarely call her Margaret. More often than not, I call her "Beautiful." Maybe it's cheesy, but I want my wife to know that I think she is gorgeous and I appreciate it. If other people snicker or laugh, that's just fine.

As husbands we are also called to love our wives—not as we want to be loved, but as she needs to be loved (which means cherished and adored). This is probably the hardest thing to do on a day-to-day basis. No one is likeable all the time, and when I get tired or stressed I definitely have to work at not pointing out all her imperfections. I have a very harsh tongue, and it has caused a lot more heartache in our home than pretty much any other character flaw I've got. In the midst of throwing myself a pity party, I've said some really hurtful things that I've immediately regretted. I usually don't want to admit that I'm wrong, which just exacerbates the situation. Eventually, I look at her and see the pain and hurt I've caused, and I ask for her forgiveness. As I reflect back on these incidents even now, I'm reminded that when I allow myself to act like this I'm not being loving towards my wife. When I see how I hurt her, I am reminded that I must hurt Christ even more frequently with my rotten, selfish behavior.

Thankfully, because of grace, I am able to have a relationship with both Jesus and my wife. For that I am grateful.

Guarding My Eyes, Protecting Her Heart

The final thing I'd like to point out is an area of weakness for many men, including myself. I've struggled with the temptation to view pornography for a large part of my life. Though I'd love to tell you that the instant I was married the temptation disappeared, if I did I'd be lying. The temptation for lust is strong; and it has been only by the prayers of my wife, studying the promises of Scripture, and recognizing times of potential weakness that I've been able to battle this.

Here is what I've discovered about myself: Just as I lose control of my tongue when I am tired or stressed, I am also weakest in those times to the temptation of lust. With that knowledge I've been able to set some boundaries for myself that are pivotal in my quest to becoming a godly man and husband for my wife.

The boundaries I have set up include checking my personal email in the middle of the day or in the evening when Margaret is around, not watching TV late at night when all the real crud comes on, and taking the extra minute to review why a movie is rated what it is before I rent it. Of course, nothing is perfect. Sometimes I get hit with a blast of lust for no apparent reason or I slip and make a bad decision. In those instances I rely on the love that both Christ and Margaret have for me and tell them both what has happened. It is never good for my pride, but the honesty has made me a less judgmental person toward others who struggle with different sins.

The other principle I recognize is that having a thought for a second and dwelling on it are two very different things. When I'm hit with a thought that a woman other than my wife is attractive, I try to tell my wife about it as soon as possible. After we discuss the situation, I'll do whatever it takes to make sure Margaret knows I am honoring her even when I'm around other women I might find attractive.

I pray God uses some of the mistakes I have made to help you become the man He has called you to be. May the grace and peace of God our Father and the Lord Jesus Christ guide you and your wife as you navigate the first years of marriage together.

Quick Tip: Arrange a weekend getaway.

Questions for Reflection

1. How well do you know your wife? When was the last time you intentionally tried to learn something new about her likes and dislikes?

2. How do you see God using you and your wife together in ministry? What steps are you taking to help you grow spiritually together?

3. Is there anything you haven't been honest with your wife about? How can you be more honest with her on a day-to-day basis?

4. What steps are you taking to protect yourself from sexual temptation? Are they working? Do you need to take any other steps?

For Her Only—Being the Best Spouse You Can Be

thirteen

As God's chosen people,
holy and dearly loved,
clothe yourselves with com-
passion, kindness, humility,
gentleness and patience.

—COLOSSIANS 3:12-13

IN THE MOVIE *ABOUT SCHMIDT,* WARREN SCHMIDT (played by Jack Nicholson), finds himself at a crossroads in life. Shortly after his retirement, he loses his wife and must marry off his daughter to a less-than-desirable suitor. The film follows his journey of self-discovery across the country in a newly purchased 35-foot motor home. Reflecting on his marriage of 42 years, Warren asks himself a startlingly deep and reflective question: Did his wife, Helen, really love him or did she merely put up with him for the last four decades?

It's a question that many men, including your husband, quietly wonder. Do you *really* love him? Beyond his income potential, strength, wit, waist and hairline, do you *really* love him?

Your heart screams yes, but don't be surprised when from time to time he looks at you with wonder. At those moments you have an opportunity to affirm him in your adoration. Generally, when couples first fall in love, they are willing to compliment each other around the clock. Remember when you first noticed the strength of his hands, the piercing color of his eyes, the cuteness of his (fill in the blank). As time goes on, it is easy to assume he already knows you love him, like him, and adore him. And besides, what you really need him to do now is take out the trash, mow the lawn, pay the bills, or (fill in the blank). Let me let you in on a secret: The only way your husband is going to know you're still enamored with him is if you tell him.

Express your love. Hide a card in his suitcase. Tuck a note in the shower. Write on a steam-covered mirror after you bathe. Take a few moments to grab him by the shoulders, look into his eyes, and tell him you love him. It's so obvious yet so easy to leave undone.

Make sure you don't just praise him on things he does, but on who he is. Take note of his appearance, the way he carries himself, and those Christlike moments when he gives, serves, or responds with grace.

Let Him Know Your Needs

You want him to read your mind. You expect him to read your mind. You pray he will be able to read your mind. We all do. But do you know what? He cannot do it. Sure, he can get lucky every so often, but if you're waiting for your husband to have a "Eureka!" moment when he suddenly understands you, you're going to grow old waiting. If you don't tell your spouse what you *really* want and need, then you're inviting him to become insensitive to you.

SURPRISE NO. 21

My husband will never be able to read my mind.

Part of what your husband loves about you is that he doesn't get you. He loves that there is something mysterious, wild, and untouchable about you. He loves that every time he thinks he has you all figured out, you throw him for a loop. He loves your spontaneity. He loves your pizzazz. He loves your sparkle. He loves that you keep him on his toes.

More than anything, your spouse wants to make you happy. Few things bring a bigger smile to his face, but he's not going to be able to do it if you don't share your needs. So forget about him developing a sixth sense that instantly tells him when you're happy, moody, or upset. Let him know what you're thinking, feeling, and desiring. Maybe you need to hear "I love you" every night before bed, get fresh flowers once a week, or find cards left around the house. Maybe you need a getaway weekend, the cell phone turned off during dinner, or to spend the next holiday with your family. Drop the guessing games and let him know—point blank—what you (and he) really want.

No Mo' Nitpicking and Nagging

Some things have to be done. Some things need to be done. Some things should be done. And some things will never get done. As a wife you're going to spend an amazing amount of time waiting for your spouse to do something: file a claim with health insurance, take the car in for a tune-up, or clip the hedges. How you respond to waiting will determine whether you're a nag.

Rather than remind your spouse every day or hour about what needs to get done, consider making a honey-do list. Record the items that need to get done and highlight or note the ones that are priorities. That way your husband can go to a third party—a list—to find out what needs to be done rather than having a verbal reminder of jobs left undone whenever he sees you.

Quick Tip: Pray together at least once every day.

In order to avoid nitpicking, you really need to pick your battles. Your husband is naturally going to have things about him that drive you nuts. Maybe he puts his clothes on the floor beside the laundry hamper or never bothers to clear the shower drain of clumps of hair. Maybe he cracks his knuckles or hums when he puts on deodorant in the morning. Little idiosyncrasies can eventually get the best of you, so be on guard to pick your battles and let some of them go. Focusing on the small issues and becoming a nitpicker will only steal the joy marriage is designed to bring you. So the next time your husband begins to do that little thing that's annoying, take a second look—isn't there something about it that's kind of cute?

Spark the Romance

Sex is too good to allow it to become predictable. I'll never forget my newlywed friend Renee, who confessed that she was surprised how early in their marriage sex became as predictable as turning on the coffeepot in the morning. "After dinner we'd watch television, have sex, and go to bed," she says. "I expected it to be a little more tantalizing a little longer."

Do you remember the film *Groundhog Day?* In the movie Bill Murray woke up to the same day over and over. Sex can become like *Groundhog Day* if you're not careful. It can become rote. Fortunately, all it takes is a little creativity to spice things ups. Pick out a new piece of lingerie or borrow one of his shirts. Put on that black or pink bra and panty. Simple things, such as changing the time of day, lighting, or position, can make things more interesting. Add candles, music, or massage oils. Buy a new book on sex—and read it (together)!

Don't forget the power of smooching. When was the last time you two just had a good make-out session—no sex required? Long, passionate kisses have a way of reigniting intense emotions. Get in the car if you need to. One friend I know who has six kids took her husband by the hand after eight years of marriage and led him out to the driveway one night after the children were settled for a touchy-feely good time in their 15-passenger van. They even steamed up the windows!

Don't forget to flirt. Pinch his butt. Walk by with a sexy stroll. Wink at him from across the room. Let him know you're interested. The good news is that it doesn't take a whole lot to spark the romance.

Don't Forget to Play

You may consider yourself a wife, companion, helpmate, or mother. Don't forget one of the most powerful titles you've been given: playmate. You are your husband's best friend. What do best friends do together? Have fun! It's easy to forget the fun factor underneath the never-ending pile of bills, responsibilities, and mortgage payments. Your husband wants to have fun with you, so make sure to give the fun stuff a chance.

Dust off the board games. Pull out the Ping-Pong table. Put on your hiking shoes. When was the last time you went bowling together? Visited an amusement park? Attended a children's concert? Enjoyed ice cream cones with too many toppings?

SURPRISE NO. 22

You just can't have too much fun. In fact, Dr. Howard Markman, author of *Fighting for Your Marriage*, reports that the amount of fun couples had together was the single strongest factor in their overall marital happiness. So learn what makes your partner laugh. Crack jokes. Have a pillow fight. Play tag. Run around barefoot. Create notes with clues for hidden surprises around the house. Tackle each other with affection.

Part of being a playmate is being able to do nothing together. Remember the show *Seinfeld*? It was a show about nothing in particular and life in general. As a playmate, you can have fun doing nothing with your spouse. Spend time on the couch reading books. Visit a library and enjoy the magazine section together. Sit on a park bench and watch the world go by. Play. Enjoy. Laugh.

Tame Those Emotions

Hormonal fluctuations are part of a woman's life that most men will never understand. They are both complex and compelling. They have the strength to overpower our rational side and take us into a realm where what we feel in our heart compels us to take action over what we know in our head. Emotions can result in uncontrollable laughter and blissful glee as well as heartfelt tears and hurt. God enriched all of our lives by giving us great emotional capacity, but we need to be wary of allowing emotions—which can be as unpredictable as the ocean during *The Perfect Storm*—to rule our lives. If left untamed, emotions can cause us to become bitter, hurtful, and harmful toward ourselves and our spouse.

A small verse in Galatians provides some insight into taming our emotions. It says, "So I say, live by the Spirit, and you will not gratify the desires of the sinful nature" (Galatians 5:16). This verse invites us to live a life directed by Christ rather than by our own whims and fancies. It asks us to turn to God and be led by the Holy Spirit rather than relying on our own impulsive responses. To put it simply, we are asked to respond to God's prompting rather than immediately react to a situation.

What does this look like? It may mean giving yourself a time-out. What do many parents do when a child misbehaves? They give the child a time-out for a few minutes as both punishment and to provide time for the child to figure out what he or she has done wrong. Sometimes I need a time-out. My grace is gone. My patience is spent. I am about to unleash some fury. It is at this point that I need to choose to sit down and cool off. It's during this time that I can transform my fuming at someone or a situation into prayer toward God. My prayers may even be angry when I begin, but at least I am fuming in the right direction, and God is given the opportunity to begin working on my heart. During my time-out I can make sure I am not allowing my emotions to get the best of me and seek a more godly response.

Another important aspect of taming your emotions is simply knowing your own body. Every month about the same time, I disqualify myself from making any major decisions. While some doctors still debate the validity of PMS, my husband and I are in the camp that says it's real. During those few days leading up to my cycle, I am not fully rational. I am not fully sound. I can still think, function, hold a conversation, and cook a meal or two, but my senses are heightened. An issue that would be a little thing any other time of the month becomes a really big thing. To ensure I don't take my emotions out on my husband, I try to give Leif a heads-up that it is coming. Then he knows to give me greater grace if I have a short fuse or act a little batty.

Emotions can get the best of us as women. They are an enormous strength and have the power to motivate, compel, and embrace like none other. They can also make our husbands feel that they're in a no-win situation. Nothing they say can make it better. If you find yourself on an emotional roller coaster, you may need to visit a doctor and/or change your diet to help bring yourself back to an even keel.

Don't Make Fun

One of the quickest ways to hurt your spouse and undermine your relationship is to make fun of him. Little put-downs, snide remarks, and verbal picking on him do an amazing amount of damage to a relationship and harm your ability to be intimate and open with your spouse. Even if you can control your tongue, be aware that you need to avoid a physical response—such as rolling your eyes or shrugging your shoulder as if you don't care. These physical responses will show that you don't respect what he has to say. He is more sensitive in this one area than you can ever imagine.

Why is this so crucial? Because when you don't respect your spouse, you don't listen to your spouse. When people don't listen to each other, communication breaks down and conflict inevitably follows.

Questions for Reflection

1. How often do you fall into the trap of expecting your spouse to read your mind? What steps can you take to be more honest about what you're thinking and feeling?

2. What topics are you most likely to nag your spouse about? What do you need to do to decrease the nagging factor?

3. When was the last time you had a play day with your husband? What would a fun day together look like? When can you schedule it?

4. Is there a time of the month or year when hormones get the best of you? What can you do to make sure you don't take out any hormonal fluctuations on your husband?

Finding God (Again) After You've Found Your Mate

fourteen

*When was the last time you
looked at your mate watching TV,
maybe with a beer in his hand,
and thought,* He is made in the
image and likeness of God? *When
was the last time you pressed
warmly against your mate,
knowing she is made in the image
and likeness of God—and not just
a body there for your amusement?
What a difference a divine image
can make in a marriage.*

—MICHAEL SHEVACK

EVEN BEFORE LEIF AND I TIED THE KNOT, we were committed to growing together spiritually. We had high aspirations. Maybe you had them too.

Early in our dating career, Leif started a habit of praying for me before we separated each night. If we were apart, he would pray over the phone. The prayer was pulled straight from Scripture. Known as the Aaronic Blessing (after Aaron, Moses' brother), it says:

> The LORD bless you and keep you;
> The LORD make His face shine upon you,
> And be gracious to you;
> The LORD lift up His countenance upon you,
> And give you peace (Numbers 6:24-26 NKJV).

It turns out that the prayer was the same one his parents had prayed over him every night while growing up. In addition to this prayer, we made a commitment to pray together every day. That lasted about a week. Then, a few days after Christmas, we decided to make a New Year's resolution to read a devotional together. We selected Oswald Chamber's *My Utmost for His Highest*. By mid-February, we were two weeks behind. We tried to catch up, but by the beginning of March, we knew it was a lost cause.

In the spring we decided to read a book together called *Talking Donkeys and Wheels of Fire: Bible Stories That Are Truly Bizarre* by J. Stephen Lang. Loaded with fun, easy-to-read chapters about unusual events and encounters in the Bible, we are still only halfway through the book a year later. We have also tried buying two copies of a book—*Boundaries in Marriage* by Henry Cloud and John Townsend, which we have heard is wonderful. Our original goal was to read them simultaneously, but I don't think either of us is past the first chapter, despite our aspirations.

SURPRISE NO. 23

Connecting spiritually as a couple on a consistent basis is more challenging than I ever anticipated.

More than a year into marriage and two years into our relationship, we are still trying to determine what works for us as a couple. The only thing we've discovered so far is that what works for other couples generally hasn't worked for us. So we're still experimenting and trying new ways to grow together spiritually. We have discovered a few things that have worked. First and foremost, that little Aaronic blessing has become an indispensable part of our lives. Every night Leif prays that prayer over me. Some nights we say it together, and other nights I pray it back over him. He usually places his hand on my forehead, thanks to a little urging, and it is one of the sweetest moments of the day. If we're in different cities, then he'll pray it over the phone or send it an email. That little prayer reminds us each day who is really in control of our lives and our marriage. It also helps us to deal with any issues that have been left on the back burner all day. It's hard to sincerely pray for someone—even if it's a memorized prayer—when you're angry with the person. Thus, the prayer has become a check in our lives to make sure we don't let the sun set on our anger. Sometimes we'll find ourselves talking about issues before we can pray, and occasionally we'll have to deal with them afterward.

While I've never been a fan of rote prayers, I have found that the commitment to this simple prayer time often launches us into a deeper prayer time in which we pray for each other, situations, and loved ones in our lives. We will find ourselves batting prayers back and forth and praying for one another in unexpected ways.

On several occasions Leif and I have tried reading a portion of Scripture together and discussing its meaning. This process has been hit-and-miss for us. Occasionally we'll be able to launch into a deep discussion, but other times we find ourselves struggling to connect. We have found that one person reading Scripture out loud can be helpful. Whether it's a psalm, proverb, story from one of the Gospels, or short passage from the Epistles, it can be powerful to hear the Scriptures read aloud by your mate. Sometimes when I am discouraged or ill, Leif will simply read a few chapters from the book

Quick Tip: Be playful.

of Psalms over me. It's one of the most comforting and encouraging things he can do.

Both Leif and I love reading Christian books, but we're not very good at sharing a book. We both tend to want to read at odd times in odd places, and tracking down a shared book can be a frustrating experience. Instead, we're learning to recommend a book that we've read to one another. I recently read *Ordering Your Private World* by Gordon MacDonald, a book that had a great impact on my spiritual and personal life. Leif read it afterward, and we were able to sort through many of the issues it raised. Leif recently picked up a book called *Corporate Giants* by Robert Darden and P.J. Richardson that he was jazzed about, so now I'm making my way through its pages. While we don't always read the same books—he prefers fiction and I prefer nonfiction—we offer each other summaries of the titles we read and use them as discussion starters.

Another place we delve into spiritual issues is at the movie theater. Films raise all kinds of spiritual issues, including redemption, forgiveness, good vs. evil, hope, love, and courage. After we sit through a movie—and we usually stay through all the credits, which can be fascinating—we'll take time to talk about what we just saw. After watching *Spider-Man 2*, we talked about the issues of purpose, identity, and self-sacrifice. After enjoying *Big Fish*, we talked about the role of exaggeration in storytelling and its ethical implications. Granted, we didn't find too many deep issues in *Dumb and Dumber* because some movies are just meant to be fun, but it can be rewarding to find the God-themes together in film.

We have also developed a habit of keeping the Sabbath together. Leif and I both consider work our play—which qualifies us as workaholics. It's wonderful to love what you do, but we constantly battle becoming what we do and having our identity wrapped up in our professions.

Quick Tip: Remember that no one is perfect—including you.

One of the ways we combat this trend is by taking one day off a week. If our schedules allow and since we go to church on Saturday nights, we'll usually take Sunday off, but if there's a conflict, we'll try to reschedule for any other day that is available. The main focus of the day is rest. We'll sleep in, snuggle in bed, and then make our way to the living room, where we will listen to a downloaded sermon from one of our favorite Bible teachers—Rob Bell of Mars Hill Bible Church in Grand Rapids, Michigan.

We'll talk about the message and then take some time to read our Bibles or a spiritual title before making lunch. During the afternoon, we'll usually go for a walk, take a nap, or watch a movie. In the evening we attend a relaxed small group to enjoy Christian fellowship with friends. We try to get in bed by 10 P.M., so we can get a good night's rest before the workweek kicks off Monday morning.

This one day has become a physical, spiritual, and mental sanctuary in our lives. It draws our hearts back to God and each other and reminds us we are so much more than what we do. Some Sabbaths I'll find myself drawn to prayer, repentance, or simply staring out the window enjoying the wonder of God's creation. These holy moments have become the highlight of my week.

Yet taking a day off is a constant battle for both of us. All kinds of events and scheduling conflicts try to snuff out our precious day of rest, and we find ourselves constantly fighting to make the time for the day off. People will call and invite us to birthday parties, ask us to help them move, or request that we get involved in an activity of some sort. We've become very intentional about guarding this time, but it has been worth it.

Being intentional is at the heart of any growth we've had together spiritually. Before I was married, I had this picture in my mind that my husband and I would just grow spiritually together by simply being together. But it's taken so much more. It takes intentional effort.

It requires turning off the television, shifting the focus of the conversation, and placing worship albums by the CD player. It requires creating a home and a relationship that is conducive to growth. Most importantly, it requires growing on your own time.

Finding God Again

Before I was married, I didn't have any problems getting up in the morning and spending time reading my Bible and praying. I had a regular time and place where I met with God, and it worked quite well until I wasn't alone anymore.

Suddenly I didn't just have God to wake up to in the morning; I had a spouse—a wonderful, cute, warm, snuggly spouse. Just his presence made me want to lie in bed for hours and cuddle. Eventually one of us would volunteer to make breakfast for the other, and then we were planning our day. Groceries to buy. Errands to run. People to see. Before I knew it, my husband and I were sitting down to dinner, and I hadn't spent any time with God.

The worst part was that this kind of day wasn't unusual; it was quickly becoming the norm. I'd find myself cracking open my Bible to read a few verses during a few

Growing Together Spiritually

Here are a few activities to try to jump-start your spiritual lives together. If one doesn't work, don't beat yourself up about it. Simply try another:

- Read a devotional such as *Daily Bread* together.
- Pray in the mornings or before bed together.
- Try memorizing Scripture together.
- Read a Christian book together.
- Create a place—whether it's a particular chair or couch—that is conducive to quiet times.
- Make time to pray together, even if it's over the phone.
- Read the Bible together and discuss.
- Look for spiritual themes in films, books, and music.
- Carve time out of your schedule for both of you to focus on spending that time with God.
- Go on a retreat.
- Choose a day to fast together.
- Pray together about a particular issue every day for a week.
- Play worship music in your home.
- Download sermons from some of your favorite Bible teachers.

spare moments or turning on the local radio station to catch portions of a sermon while driving to the grocery store. The once-intimate relationship I had with Jesus was becoming stale. I was having a hard time juggling my relationship with God and the relationship with my spouse.

It's something I still struggle to balance. I finally talked about the issue with my husband, and we decided that we would give each other more time and space to grow spiritually. This means that after cuddling time and before breakfast, we give each other time to read our Bibles. Or maybe one person reads while the other scrambles eggs. We have both had to become more deliberate with our free time too. In our infrequent down moments, I need to resist the urge to watch VH1's "I Love The 90s" and spend some time in prayer. Some days it's tough—especially when I just want brainless activity. Yet the rewards of seeking God are incomparable.

I am slowly learning that if I am going to love my spouse as God calls me to love him, then I have to seek God first. That is the highest priority. As much as I want to love my spouse on my own—and on a gushy, mushy, ga-ga-in-love day I really feel I can—I need God to permeate me with His unconditional love if I am ever going to be able to extend it to my husband. It's only through Him that the fullness of God's love can be made known, and that simple truth helps me realize my true priorities.

Sarah, a 22-year-year old, says a lot of married couples bring false expectations of what their spiritual lives will look like when they're married. "You have this one-on-one relationship with Jesus, and you try to bring in this third person and it doesn't work like you think it's going to work," she says.

Sarah's husband, Peter, is very disciplined in his approach to knowing God. Every morning, Peter wakes up at 6 A.M. to spend an hour or more studying and praying. "He's very disciplined," Sarah says. "I might try to do it for a week, but I'm not a morning person

Quick Tip: Sit on the porch or deck together and enjoy each other.

and eventually I'll stop. Peter's big strength is reading the Bible and studying. Mine is prayer, so it's been neat bringing those things together, but I struggle feeling guilty for not reading the Bible more. It's been hard for me. When we were just friends and dating, we would have quiet times together, and they were awesome. I had this picture of what it would be like once we were married, and now we're in real lives doing different things and I think, *Why isn't it like that?*"

Besides struggling with expectations and comparisons, many couples also struggle to connect with God in the same way. Anna, a 28-year-old who has been married for two years, says she and her husband don't relate to God exactly the same: "A lot of it has to do with the way we were raised. I was in an intellectual church, and his has been more Spirit-oriented," she says. "How do you blend those? We try to get together and have a Bible study or time of worship, and one will think it was awesome and the other will think, *That was dumb* or *What's the point?* That's the hardest thing—not being on the same page spiritually. We represent both of those extremes, and yet we think that will be part of our ministry one day."

Anna says she and her husband are learning to appreciate each other's spiritual backgrounds and traditions, and they are learning to develop some of their own traditions together.

It can be challenging when your spouse doesn't relate to God in the same way you do, but it can also be enriching. What can you learn from your spouse's relationship with God? What can you learn from the way your spouse worships, prays, or studies the Bible? What aspects of God does your spouse have a real grasp on—reverence, awe, relationship—that you could gain from?

One of the most encouraging things about pursuing God in marriage is that God can begin to lead you as a spouse. Sometimes it's a bit challenging, but it's always good. I remember one night last winter when Leif and I were about to go to bed, and he decided to

Quick Tip: Never forget that you and your spouse are a team.

check email at the last minute. While he said it would just take a moment, he was gone for more than 20 minutes. I lay in bed fuming.

I finally got up and turned all the lights off in the living room and bedroom and pretended to fall asleep. Even in my anger, I could hear the still, quiet voice inside my spirit whisper, "Turn the lights back on." I knew that is what I was supposed to do. I knew I was supposed to be patient with my husband, but at the moment I really didn't care. I lay in bed. A little while later I heard a thud as my husband made his way across the dark living room.

Then he came in the bedroom and turned on the light. Not only had he banged his ankle, but also he wanted to know why I had left him in the dark. It took nearly 30 minutes to sort out the issue, but at the core of it all was my own selfishness. I found myself apologizing and regretting that I hadn't listened to the quiet nudge of the Holy Spirit.

The fact is that God will lead and direct our marriages if we'll let Him and listen to Him. He desires to lead us—not only as individuals but also as a couple—beside still waters and restore our souls (Psalm 23). Yet it takes a listening ear and obedience to respond to His loving invitation.

Questions for Reflection

1. How has your relationship with God changed now that you're married?

2. What spiritual disciplines have been easy to maintain since you got married? Which have been challenging to maintain?

3. In what areas are you and your spouse able to grow together spiritually?

4. How do your different backgrounds enhance your ability to serve and worship God together?

Words of Wisdom

"Don't try and make your spouse into what you want them to be. Accept them and pray for God's best in their life. That took the pressure off of my expectations and put them in God's hands. Don't wait until the boiling point before discussing matters that concern you. Listen to each other carefully...don't jump to conclusions. Respect what your spouse has to say even if you do not agree."

—Sharon, married 36 years

"I try to be at the door when Jeremy walks in from a long day. I give him a quick squeeze, kiss, and greeting to let him know I'm glad to see him and then let him do what he needs to do while I continue with what I had been working on. This has been my way of showing that I'm glad he is home, yet willing to let him do what he needs to. He can feel loved and welcomed into our home without pressure to conform to any one mode."

—Kara, married four months

"If I could give a young couple any advice about communication, it would be to do what we didn't do: Have a regular devotion time together and pray together, not just over big things, but about things at church, at work, between each other, families, and so on. I wish we had developed that habit. And it doesn't have to be a daily thing...a few times a week or even once a week is better than none at all."

—Beth, married 30 years

"When we are upset with each other and trying to resolve something, my husband pulls me close and hugs me, and bad feelings melt away quite quickly in that position."

—Renee, married one year and four months

... continued

"Leave love notes for each other in surprising places. It's amazing what that can do!"

—Leslie, married two and a half years

"I am realizing that for me to be a healthy half of the relationship, it is a priority that we make time for ourselves. I've noticed how easy it is to get wrapped up in work or social gatherings and not spend any quality time alone with my husband. Just because we are together isn't good enough—sometimes we have to make the extra effort to make that time quality."

—Erynn, married six months

"Hanging out with people who have inspiring marriages replenishes us."

—Jonathon, married 27 years

"Don't take your husband for granted. The unique bonding together of a couple is one of the miracles God has for us in marriage. The longer you are married, the closer you begin to think, feel, discern, and hear from each other what the Lord is saying. Cherish your relationship because you don't know how many years you'll have."

—Renee, married 38 years

Was I Really Married at an Altar?

fifteen

Above all, love each other deeply, because love covers over a multitude of sins.

—1 PETER 4:8

THE OPENING SCENE OF A HUGH GRANT MOVIE is set in an airport. The character played by Hugh Grant tells us that whenever he wonders about love, he takes a detour to an airport terminal, where he can watch people who have been separated for a period of time embrace each other. As the camera scans the people—young and old—hugging, laughing, and smiling, the film lays out its very simple but powerful premise: Love is all around.

Sooner or later you'll stumble upon days in your marriage when you may need to hop in your car and visit your local airport to remind yourself that love is real and that affection, caring, selflessness, kindness, and rich relationships abound.

Wrestling with Selfishness

Learning to live with another person can be hard, especially if you're older, and especially if you're not used to asking permission for something or being held accountable for your actions.

Marriage has a unique way of revealing our selfishness and desire for self-preservation. Anyone who has ever been married for more than a month knows that both partners giving 50 percent to "make it work" doesn't add up to a 100 percent satisfying marriage. Hardly. It requires both partners giving 100 percent. That means that at times we will both do the dishes, take out the trash, and even make sure the oil in the car gets changed (gasp!). And this means not being able to buy exactly what you wanted with the money you earned.

Marriage has revealed my own self-centeredness. Recently, my husband and I were talking about where we'd like to take a vacation together in the fall. I suggested that we go back to the place where I had been married. I actually said "where *I* had been married"!

My husband called me on the carpet: "You mean where *we* got married."

I blushingly agreed.

It's so easy for my life to be about me, but it's not. Marriage has an amazing way of reminding me of this truth.

SURPRISE NO. 24

Marriage is a constant reminder that it's not about me.

If life is an onion, then marriage requires us to peel off some layers of ourselves. It requires that we put someone ahead of ourselves—not just for a day or a week, but for a lifetime. This is one of God's most clever designs to prompt us to die to self, sacrifice, and grow. Marriage invites us to become more compassionate, kind, and loving even when it hurts. It gives us the opportunity not just to reflect on 1 Corinthians 13, but also to put this epic definition of love into practice on a daily basis. Can you remember the last time you reflected on the words of this section of Scripture?

If I speak in the tongues of men and of angels, but have not love, I am only a resounding gong or a clanging cymbal. If I have the gift of prophecy and can fathom all mysteries and all knowledge, and if I have a faith that can move mountains, but have not love, I am nothing. If I give all I possess to the poor and surrender my body to the flames, but have not love, I gain nothing.

Love is patient, love is kind. It does not envy, it does not boast, it is not proud. It is not rude, it is not self-seeking, it is not easily angered, it keeps no record of wrongs. Love does not delight in evil but rejoices with the truth. It always protects, always trusts, always hopes, always perseveres. Love never fails.

But where there are prophecies, they will cease; where there are tongues, they will be stilled; where there is knowledge, it will pass away. For we know in part and we prophesy in part, but when perfection comes, the imperfect disappears. When I was a child, I talked like a child, I thought like a child, I reasoned like a child. When I became a man, I put childish ways behind me. Now we see but a poor reflection as in a mirror; then we shall see face to face. Now I know in part; then I shall know fully, even as I am fully known.

And now these three remain: faith, hope and love. But the greatest of these is love (1 Corinthians 13).

One of the healthiest exercises I've ever done is to insert my own name in the verses every time the word "Love" or "it" (referring to love) is used in the second portion of the chapter. Try using your name.

> (Your name) is patient, (Your name) is kind. (Your name) does not envy, (Your name) does not boast, (Your name) is not proud. (Your name) is not rude, (Your name) is not self-seeking, (Your name) is not easily angered, (Your name) keeps no record of wrongs. (Your name) does not delight in evil but rejoices with the truth. (Your name) always protects, always trusts, always hopes, always perseveres. (Your name) never fails.

When this Scripture is personalized, we get a vision of what Christ wants to accomplish in and through us as His disciples. We see the rough spots God wants to work out of our life as we slowly die to the things of our sinful nature and are resurrected in the life that is in Him. God often uses marriage to bring about parts of that death, and thus the altar becomes a place not only where we get married, but also where we die to self.

There are so many times in my marriage when I am tempted to be selfish. Whether I'm cooking a meal—and want the less burned piece of meat for myself—or justifying an expense that is really about my pleasure rather than my actual needs, my selfish nature has a way of rearing its ugly head. I find myself thinking about me, what I want, what makes me comfortable, what pleases me—everything me-centered.

Marriage comes along and demands that you look outward—toward someone else—if the relationship is going to be healthy and successful. Marriage asks that I do the dishes for the fiftieth time, get up and drop whatever I'm doing when my spouse walks in the door after a long day's work, and respond with love when my

Quick Tip: Remember that the Golden Rule applies to your spouse.

favorite vase gets knocked over during an animated conversation. Love asks that I respond with compassion rather than anger, pride, or self-righteousness. Love translates itself into the details of life. It invites me to let my spouse drink the last Dr Pepper and watch *Fear Factor*.

Love also invites humility. It asks that I communicate when I want to shut down. It requires that I forgive when I want to tally the wrongs and forget when I want to tally up who did what for whom. Love asks that I remain patient even when I don't have the time. Love—true love fashioned after God's love for us—has the power to transform me from everything I am into everything I was called to become.

Yet I cannot lay hold of the thing called "love" apart from the One who designed and displayed love in the beginning. God's invitation when we are at our worst is to redeem us into His best. Thus, when my heart grows cold, stale, and crisp with the frigidness of my selfish nature, God warms the core of my being with a life like no other—His life that impregnates me with faith, hope, love, grace, goodness, and all else that I do not possess in myself. God uses marriage—the very gift He gives us—to transform us, grow us, and display Himself in our lives.

As Harville Hendrix, Ph.D, observes, "Something I've learned is that real life is counterinstinctual. We're designed as creatures to protect ourselves and to survive, and therefore we go after what we need. But with real love, you commit to the survival of the other person."*

SURPRISE NO. 25

The more you die to yourself,
the more you experience real life.

FOOTNOTE

* From *O Magazine*, "Love: The Verb," February 2004, p. 175.

Marriage gives us the opportunity to grow beyond our wildest dreams. Jesus said the greatest commands were to love God with our entire beings and love our neighbors as ourselves. In marriage we have the opportunity to love our live-in neighbor on a day-in, day-out basis. We are given the opportunity to learn and relearn the golden rule of doing to others as we would like them to do to us.

And we are able to have our sinful nature magnified in ways that would be harder to recognize if we were still single. Marriage brings our selfish nature to the surface and unveils our pettiness, anger, and desire for self-preservation. We are also given the opportunity to learn wisdom. Over the years we learn which battles, if any, are worth fighting and discover the awesome power of grace and forgiveness.

Marriage may begin at an altar—a place traditionally known for sacrificial death—but it can quickly become a place of new life. In John 12:24, Jesus explores this theme when He says, "I tell you the truth, unless a kernel of wheat falls to the ground and dies, it remains only a single seed. But if it dies, it produces many seeds."

So the next time you find yourself with an opportunity to die to self—remember that it's through that death that God brings new life and growth.

Katherine, who has been married 30 years, says that during her marriage she's learned that her husband is ultimately not responsible for her good humor or her attitudes.

"I had to learn to forgive him for not doing everything just the way I thought it should be done and allow him some room to make mistakes," Katherine says. "I had to recognize that I'm not perfect either, and that our relationship together is way more important than the socks that don't hit the laundry basket, the newspapers left on my kitchen counter, or any number of other petty gripes."

Quick Tip: Squeeze fresh juice for your spouse one morning.

Being too uptight about those little things provides fertile soil in which a critical nature can take root and discontent can grow, and those bad attitudes will affect your emotions, sex life, communication, and countless other areas of your relationship. Katherine says, "It's just too high a cost to pay for such pettiness, and selfishness is really self-centeredness. My husband and I are both pretty generous people, but we are often tempted by the me-first, what's-in-it-for-me, what-do-I-want? attitudes."

Questions for Reflection

1. In what ways has marriage exposed your selfish nature?

2. What types of moments cause you to die to self? What is the response in your heart when you make sacrifices?

3. How has your marriage required you to grow?

4. In what ways have you grown as a married person that you wouldn't have grown in (as readily) as a single person?

Six Myths About Marriage

Myth No. 1: *Love will get us through.* Love is an essential part of a successful marriage, but it is going to take more than an emotion or feeling to keep you two together long enough to celebrate a silver or golden anniversary. You need realistic expectations about yourself, your spouse, and your future. You need healthy communication. And, more importantly, you need faith. A vibrant relationship with God and a rich prayer life will do more to infuse your marriage with vibrancy than you can imagine.

Myth No. 2: *Sex is going to be the easy part of marriage.* While sex can be one of the best parts of being married, it can also be one of the most challenging. Learning to understand, respond to, and please your partner takes time. If you were sexually active before you were married, you may find yourself sorting through some unwanted baggage. If you waited to have sex until you were married, you may be surprised at how much practice it takes to have a consistently enjoyable experience.

Myth No. 3: *Marriages today don't last.* It's true that more than half of all marriages today don't last, but that doesn't mean that yours has to be one of them. By basing your relationship on one nonnegotiable—divorce is not an option—you will become part of a generation that embraces the richness of marriage.

Myth No. 4: *Fights are bad for a marriage.* While there's no place for physical or emotional abuse in a relationship, there has to be room for disagreement. When you disagree with your spouse, you have the opportunity to grow, get to know your partner, and compromise. If you learn to fight fair, disagreements can strengthen you as a couple.

... continued

five Myth No. 5: *Marriage will make you happy.* It's easy to think that marriage is the passport to living happily ever after, but recent research shows that married people are often equally as happy as they were when they were single. In other words, if you were happy as a single, you'll probably be happy as a married person; but if you were unhappy while you were single, there's a good chance you'll bring that into the relationship. It's been observed, "Marriage isn't supposed to make you happy; it's supposed to make you married."

six Myth No. 6: *Children will bring us together.* Some spouses, especially women, believe that if they're going through a tough spot in their relationship, having a child will bring them together. While the process of pregnancy and having a child is an enormous opportunity for celebration and growth, it also adds stress on a relationship. Financial stress, emotional stress, and exhaustion often set in as a couple's world is turned upside down with the arrival of the new member. If your relationship is struggling, talk to your spouse and older Christian couples for wisdom and advice. You may want to pursue counseling. Just make sure you two are on the same page before you bring someone else into the family.

sixteen | Oh, Baby—This Is Going to Change Our Life!

*You know that children
are growing up when they
start asking questions
that have answers.*

—JOHN J. PLOMP

WHENEVER I THINK ABOUT HAVING CHILDREN, I can't help but think of Cheerios. In my experience children have always been neurologically linked with the scent of cereal and crackers. I have yet to see a mom who isn't equipped with at least one backup bag of saltines, Triscuits, or breakfast cereal that is ready to go when the first sign of hunger shows on a child's face or in a child's actions. I've done enough nannying to know how many of these carbo-delights you can stuff into a Ziploc bag before they begin to break.

Like you, Leif and I have spent a lot of time talking about having children. You almost have to talk about it, not only because it's a good idea to communicate, but also because everyone you know seems to be interested in the topic too. Once the confetti is thrown at your wedding, everyone's favorite question switches from "What does your dress look like?" to "When are you going to have children?"

From other people's reactions, there seem to be wrong answers to such simple questions as, "How many kids do you want to have?"

"I don't know" doesn't seem to go over well as an answer, so you have to come up with something. "We've decided to wait three to five years," has become our standard response. We've found it's not a particularly popular answer. Most people seem to want us to say that we're having children either right away or within a year's time. We promptly explain that we're not in a place in our careers or our living situation—we've been couch surfing with house-sitting jobs for the past year—where we're ready to have a baby.

Once we dodge the "What's your pregnancy plan?" question, we usually have to answer a tougher one: "How many children do you want to have?" In theory there is no wrong answer to this question, but we've learned the hard way that there actually is a wrong answer. When we say we've been thinking about having one child, it's like saying we want to have a broken child. People look at us with a slightly abhorrent expression that says, "How could you do that to your child?" In fact, I've gotten the same "Do you really think that's healthy?" response so many times that I try to steer clear of the original question.

We aren't the only ones giving the "wrong answers" to the kid questions. Couples who are considering not having any children also receive a negative response. Quickly pegged as "selfish" or "not kid-friendly," couples who choose not to have children also get their fair share of negative feedback.

On the flip side, women who want to have a lot of children can get negative feedback as well. If you say you're going to have four or more kids, you can also get a wide-eyed "Wow, you're gonna have your hands full!" response.

The truth is that there can be a lot of scary judgments made about you based on your response to the number-o'-kids question. What's funny is that my husband and I don't have a clue as to how many babies we are actually going to have. We don't even know if we can have kids, and God may just surprise us with triplets.

The great thing is that it's never too early to begin praying for the kids you're going to have one day. You can pray for wisdom in parenting, God's will as far as timing between children if you have more than one, and how God can use you to give your child a godly upbringing. Whenever you become pregnant, whether planned or a surprise, the little one will change your life and your marriage.

Chuck, a 30-something who has been married for seven years, compares becoming parents to two buddies parachuting into the middle of combat. "We talked a lot on the plane in, but right now, it's all screaming and survival," Chuck says. "It's too urgent a time to nurture our relationship [with a three-week-old]. We're in the fight of our lives. Fortunately, we're in it together."

Chuck says his new bundle of joy has turned his life upside down. "My life revolves around cries and chemicals. My life has been dramatically redefined. Basically, the baby has become more important to me than my own life. The one person I have grown to depend on and the person I trust the most [my wife] feels the same urgency as myself. We share that mission, that bond."

Though Chuck says he has less time alone with his wife, the intimacy in their relationship is still strong. "We shared one of life's ultimate common interests and experiences," he says. "She remains the most important person in my life, aside from God."

Quick Tip: Pick out the perfect card.

When asked about advice for other couples, Chuck says prayer is the key. "My parents had me when they were very young. I've had my children later in life. There is no perfect time, except God's time. Pray for the best time. Pray for God's time."

Stephanie, a 26-year-old, was only married three months when she became pregnant. The couple had felt led to stop taking birth control, and within a few weeks Stephanie was expecting.

She says it definitely added to the pressures of the first year of marriage. "You're already learning new things about each other and working out your differences, so it heightened all of that a bit. It did help us some with communication because we wanted to talk about how to raise our children. I came from a Christian home and John didn't, so we spent a lot of time talking about things to do differently or the same as our parents had."

To prepare for parenthood, the couple took a class called "Growing Kids God's Way" by Gary and Ann Marie Ezzo to help sort through the different ways they wanted to raise their children. When the child arrived, Stephanie says it opened up a "whole new can of worms" in their marriage.

"Suddenly you are tired, drained, emotional, and overwhelmed—and that's just the first half hour after delivery," she says. "We actually didn't do too badly because we had a game plan before the baby came. We just stuck to it and it worked well for us, although we had new things to argue about."

Stephanie says the lack of freedom was a big challenge. It was hard not being able to hop up, go to Target, and walk around for an hour. Meanwhile, her husband felt new pressures about providing. The arrival of the child forced John and Stephanie to learn to listen to each other and give each other breaks when either partner was at the end of their rope.

"You quickly find out your spouse's strengths and weaknesses," Stephanie says. "But you use that to your advantage. For instance,

John couldn't function after getting up at night with the baby for two nights. He was about to lose it, and it wasn't as difficult for me, so I would get up most every night with the baby, and he would only get up on nights that he didn't have to work the next day. That worked pretty well for us."

Having a baby changed just about everything in John and Stephanie's life—even the way they watch movies. "I didn't expect my view on life to change so much, but now when I watch a movie, I no longer relate to the single, young person in the movie. I am totally on the side of the parents and imagining how they must feel."

Stephanie says that even with kids—she has three now—it's essential to make time to nurture your relationship. If you can spend the first few minutes when your spouse gets home from work just sitting and talking about the day, it can set the tone for the rest of the evening. Swapping out babysitting night with another couple who has a child is another way to make time for each other even when you're on a tight budget. It's also important to have nights when the kids go to bed early so you can enjoy intimate time together.

Though children are incredibly precious and valuable, it's important not to let them take the number one position in your life—above your relationship with God or your spouse. Remember that one day they will leave the home, and your relationship with your spouse needs to be secure. Be sensitive to your spouse and recognize that your mate can become jealous of the time and attention spent on the kids. If one or both of you are in a second marriage with stepchildren, this can become especially true. Leif really loves kids, so we are both preparing for this to become an issue for us in the future.

Many parents struggle making time for God with the arrival of a child. While single, you can spend chunks of time reading your Bible, studying, and praying; but getting married and then adding little ones makes these blocks of time a lot more difficult to come by. It is okay if you only have little bits of time to spend with God

Quick Tip: Give up something you really want to do.

tucked throughout your day rather than one longer, set time. It just takes a little bit of creativity. You may find yourself praying in the shower or while waiting in the line at the grocery store, but there are snippets of time that you can still spend with Him.

Parenting also opens up new areas of study and growth to couples. You can take Bible studies and attend small groups focused on raising children. Books such as James Dobson's *Bringing Up Boys* and Lisa Whelchel's *Creative Correction* can spark conversation, while attending conferences and special church services provide an opportunity to grow together spiritually.

At the same time, raising children teaches valuable spiritual lessons. Stephanie says one of the most valuable lessons she's learned is about God's unconditional love. "I never knew God loved me so deeply," she says. "If my husband were to barge into our house, spit on me, slap me, tell me he hates me, burn the house down, and run off into the distance, our marriage would most likely be over. However, if one of my kids were to do the same thing, I would love them no less than I did before. God knows no conditions on His love for us."

Stephanie says she never would have grasped some of these truths behind unconditional love unless she had become a mom.

So there is much to look forward to in becoming a parent—no matter how many kids you decide to have together.

Questions for Reflection

1. What have you and your spouse talked about as far as children? How many kids do you plan to have? When?

2. What have you learned about the ways you were raised compared to your spouse? Have you talked about how you'll handle your different styles of parenting?

3. What can children teach you about biblical truths?

What Do You Mean We Aren't the Only Two People in the World?

seventeen

*True friendship is like
sound health; the
value of it is seldom
known until it be lost.*

—CHARLES CALEB COLTON

CONGRATULATIONS! YOU HAVE JUST MARRIED your best friend. Your spouse is everything you wanted. All yours. But what about all of your other friends? And your spouse's?

While most couples find their relationship soars shortly after matrimony, their relationships with others tend to suffer. Even close friends—including the maid or matron of honor and best man—can fall by the wayside. While it is usually unintentional, it is all too common.

Ellie and George discovered this truth the hard way. "When we first got married, all we did was hang out alone; and let me tell you, this was a mistake!" Ellie says. "When the romance fizzled and the realities of daily life kicked in, we found ourselves with no friends. Not even married friends! Why? Because we were soooo 'in love' we forgot about nurturing all parts of our lives. The reality is that friendships with people other than your spouse can only increase your maturity and growth as a person, which in turn will enhance your marriage."

SURPRISE NO. 27

After I got married, my single friends missed me.

This young couple has been married for nearly five years, and only in the last two years have they begun to develop what Ellie calls *shared relationships*. "We had single friends during the first three years of our marriage, but in the last years we've begun to share in our relationships. In other words, the friend is not just *his* or *mine*, the friendship is shared. A perfect example of this is our friend Rob. We do tons of stuff together—just the three of us. We go to the mall, movies, out to eat, play laser tag, and just hang out and talk."

Don't Forget the Singles

Newlyweds naturally become magnets for other married couples. Melanie and Jon say they spend far more time with married couples now that they're married. "We have some dear friends who are also newlyweds, so we have a lot in common," Melanie says. "We also like spending time with couples who have been married a while because we like to learn from their relationships."

During the early stages of your marriage, it's important that you don't repel your single friends. Ann and Jake make a point to spend time with friends—either together or separately—each week. Though it's not a routine or something that's always planned, they feel the time apart is healthy and instills a greater longing for each other. "Usually Saturdays are my days to spend away from my husband," Ann says. "I have a number of friends I plan things to do with on Saturdays, and sometimes they'll call me or Jake up and say that they're going to kidnap me for a while. I also see my friends on nights when my husband has to work late. I take advantage of the time I don't get to spend with Jake by spending it with my next favorite people.

"You can feel trapped if you can't get out and be away from your spouse every now and then," she adds. "Whether it's dinner or shopping or just plain, old girl talk—it has to be a part of your relationship. Oftentimes your attitude changes depending on who you are with, and it's always fun to be around the people who can make you think or act crazy or laugh at your jokes or whatever."

Guidelines

If your single friends are of the opposite sex, you might want to think twice before spending tons of free time with them. Introduce your friends to your spouse so your mate can form a relationship with them. Make very sure your spouse knows he or she is the most important person in your life, and be conscious that people are

Some Quick Advice on Maintaining Friendships

- Set guidelines between you and your husband for spending time with friends of the opposite sex.

- Inform friends of any special days—whether it's a Sunday afternoon or Thursday night—that you plan to spend solely with your husband on a regular basis.

- Try to set apart a regular time each week—whether an afternoon or evening—when you and your husband work on developing and maintaining friendships.

- Make it a point to keep in touch with friends during the first few months and years of marriage to let them know you care.

- Send Christmas cards.

- During the first six months of your marriage, organize several group activities—dinners, movies, sporting events—that allow both you and your husband to become better acquainted with each other's friends.

- Look for opportunities to incorporate friends into your daily activities.

- Think long-term. While you may be swirling in love today, don't forget to maintain and invest time into relationships outside your marriage. You'll need them for years to come.

constantly watching how you interact with other men or women. The Bible challenges believers to avoid even the appearance of evil (1 Thessalonians 5:22 KJV).

Pam Farrel, coauthor of *Love to Love You* (Harvest House), says couples need to sit down and talk about healthy boundaries. "We always encourage people not to be alone with someone of the opposite sex," she says. "If ripples hit a marriage, it can easily turn into an affair. When stress comes, it's easy to run to a familiar face or the big, strong arms of a guy friend."

It's okay to have these friendships, but be careful. Be very careful before going out alone with someone of the opposite sex, don't have long phone conversations, and be wary of comparing the person to your own spouse. Innocent friendship can become an area of temptation for either unhealthy fantasy or actual sin. The best way to handle these kinds of friendships is to try to share them with your spouse. If this is not possible, touch base with your spouse to make sure your interactions are appropriate.

Communicate with your spouse about relational boundaries. Is it okay to have lunch alone with someone of the opposite sex? Be sensitive to each other's feelings. Remember, you and your spouse are now one. You should not do anything you wouldn't feel comfortable telling each other.

SURPRISE NO. 28

Friendships with people of the opposite sex naturally change after you get married.

Maintaining and strengthening friendships after marriage takes initiative, energy, and work, but it's always worth it. Remember that true friends are a gift from God. Nurture these friendships even after you're married. There's a richness that comes with old friends. They add continuity to your life. Share your spouse's friends, but make sure your friends are always welcomed in your life too. If you move away from close friends, then keep in touch through email, letters, and Christmas cards. They require time and intentional effort—but friendships that weather 10, 20, and 30 or more years are truly treasures.

Finally, remember that while your spouse should be your best friend, your mate can't meet every need in your life. Girlfriends are an important dimension in every female's life, just as other guys are an important part of a male's life. Don't take them for granted.*

Questions for Reflection

1. How have your relationships with your friends changed since you've gotten married?

2. What can you do to maintain your ties with your single friends?

3. What boundaries do you and your spouse have in your friendships?

4. What steps have you taken to build friendships with other newlywed and veteran couples who can encourage you in your own marriage?

FOOTNOTE

*   Portions of this chapter were adapted from an article I wrote published by *Christian Bride*.

Scriptures for Reflection

"It came about when he had finished speaking to Saul, that the soul of Jonathan was knit to the soul of David, and Jonathan loved him as himself" (1 Samuel 18:1 NASB).

"A friend loves at all times" (Proverbs 17:17 NASB).

"Two are better than one because they have a good return for their labor. For if either of them falls, the one will lift up his companion. But woe to the one who falls when there is not another to lift him up" (Ecclesiastes 4:9-10 NASB).

"Greater love has no one than this, that one lay down his life for his friends" (John 15:13 NASB).

"They were continually devoting themselves to the apostles' teaching and to fellowship, to the breaking of bread and to prayer" (Acts 2:42 NASB).

The In-law Factor

eighteen

*Humor is always based on
a modicum of truth. Have
you ever heard a joke
about a father-in-law?*

—DICK CLARK

HAVE YOU EVER NOTICED HOW A SHELF LIFE doesn't exist for in-law jokes? They never seem to pass away—year after year and generation after generation. I never understood in-law jokes until I got married and learned that, as wonderful as your spouse's family may be, they will almost never compare to your own.

SURPRISE NO. 29

In-laws are no joke.

You can tell yourself "I married my spouse, not the family" over and over again, but even if you say it ten thousand times, it's simply not true. When you say "I do," you become a part of your spouse's life and your spouse's family. This can be a tough pill to swallow—especially when your new family has different values, expectations, or traditions than your own.

Stirring the Pot

A number of factors make in-law relationships more challenging than other relationships that you have had in the past. Unlike friends or coworkers who will eventually come and go, you don't really have an option of not getting along with your in-laws. Well, actually you do have that option, but it's not a good one.

OPTION A	OPTION B
Get along with your in-laws	Fight with your in-laws
Share pleasant holidays	Dread the holidays
Enjoy peaceful conversations	Have tense conversations
Learn something new	Fight with your spouse
Laugh a lot	Get angry
Have fun	Cry

It seems like a no-brainer. Option A is the obvious choice, but many couples find themselves living with Option B. In-laws become more of a burden than a blessing. It takes hard work and intentional effort to move from Option B to Option A, but it's worth the effort.

The bottom line is that your relationship with your in-laws is crucial. After all, your new mother- and father-in-law (or two of each if your spouse's parents have divorced and remarried) raised your spouse. Your new sisters- and brothers-in-law grew up together and have a history and a bond that can't be replicated—even by you. In the best scenario, your spouse's family welcomes you with open arms and immediately counts you as one of their own—immersing you into their traditions, lingo, and family life.

At times it feels completely natural and at other times completely overwhelming. You like seeing your stocking hanging by the fireplace at Christmas but quietly wonder about the strange-tasting dessert they serve on Christmas Eve (based on a recipe that has been in their family for generations). Are you going to be expected to learn to make the odd concoction and serve it to your future children?

While immediate acceptance feels like a breath of fresh air, it's a little worrisome at the same time because your new in-laws may have approved of you without really knowing you. They may have decided that whoever their son or daughter picked to marry must be a winner, so you hope you can keep up the blue-ribbon image. Both you and your in-laws want desperately to be liked by each other so everyone can avoid becoming one of those families in which people don't really get along.

When In-laws Don't Approve

If you're less fortunate, you may find yourself in a family where the in-laws never really like you and it's obvious. Your mother-in-law or father-in-law decide that you aren't their first pick early on, and despite countless attempts, you still can't win their approval. The best scenario is to hang in there and pray that with time their hearts will change.

Building a Relationship

During the first six months of marriage, my husband and I lived across the street from my new in-laws. Eager to include us in family events—since Leif's two brothers and their wives were also living in the same town—we were invited to meals or activities anywhere from two to five times a week. At first I thought the invitations were very kind and gracious, but I found that if we tried to fulfill them all, then we didn't have time to establish friendships with other people or take the time we needed to work on our own relationship.

We said no to a number of invitations due to scheduling conflicts, travel, and the need to be alone together, but I just couldn't help feeling guilty. After all, my new family was greeting me with open arms and I was too busy for them. It was also frustrating because I wanted to extend an invitation to them for a meal or get-together, but before I had the time or space to set something up, they were already inviting us over to their house. Whenever they called I let my husband respond to the request and decide if we should go. This made me feel slightly better, but the guilt still persisted.

I prayed about the issue for nearly a year. One random afternoon I had the sudden, unexplainable courage to visit my mother-in-law and talk about the situation. I'll never forget the day I walked into our living room, looked Leif in the eye, and said, "I'm talking to your mother today." I drove to her house and vulnerably shared my concern. I explained that in a relationship there has to be a natural give-and-take. I was feeling guilty on two counts: not accepting her invitations and not having the time to reciprocate.

She smiled warmly and eased my fears. She explained that when she was growing up, her house was always the center of family activity. Whenever the family got together—which was regularly—it was always at her parents' home. Now that she has her own family, it just makes sense that the tradition would continue. She also explained that she never intended for us to come over every time she invited. They just wanted us to know we were always welcome. They also didn't ever want to just invite one of their sons and his wife and have one of the other couples drive by and see their car and feel left out.

Suddenly it all made sense.

That day my mother-in-law and I made a deal: She was welcome to call as many times as she wanted, and we were welcome to decline the invitation—guilt free—whenever we needed to. Since that day my feelings about our relationship have improved tremendously.

It took me almost a year to get up the nerve to talk to my mother-in-law, but it's one of the best, and possibly the most courageous, things I have ever done.

You may feel as though you need to have a similar conversation—to clear the air, express your concerns, or take your relationship to the next level. If so, spend time in prayer beforehand. Ask God what needs to be said and what needs to be left unsaid. Focus on the importance of strengthening the relationship. Most

Quick Tip: Pray together.

importantly, be willing to understand. Your in-law probably has a different perspective on the situation than you do. Differences in family heritage, tradition, values, and communication styles can all be factors in a potential rift. By recognizing and learning to appreciate the other side of the story, you can learn to overcome, or at least live harmoniously with, the differences.

Below are a few tips for improving your relationship with your in-laws.

Avoid speaking negatively about them, especially to your spouse. As frustrating and, at times, impossible as your in-laws may be, remember that they are still your spouse's parents. The Bible commands us to "Honor your father and your mother." (Exodus 20:12). This verse can be applied to both parents and in-laws, and it comes with a promise that you will be blessed.

Recognize that proximity can play a big factor in your relationship. If you live in the same town or within an hour's drive, you may need to establish boundaries with your in-laws. Ask them to call before they drop by. Let them know when you will and won't be available. Some couples have discovered that their relationship with their in-laws actually improves after they move.

> **Five Quick Ways to Improve Your Relationship with Your In-laws**
>
> 1. Call for no reason—just to say hello.
> 2. Learn how to make a family recipe from your mother-in-law.
> 3. Take time to learn about your spouse's family history.
> 4. Avoid mentioning any disagreements or fights you are having with your spouse when you're with your in-laws.
> 5. Greet your in-laws with a hug or handshake.

If at all possible, place yourself in situations where the relationship can develop naturally. The pressure to get along with your in-laws can sometimes choke out a relationship that would have developed naturally without the "have to" factor. Try to spend time with your in-laws other than the holidays, which tend to be high-stress times. Also try to participate in activities outside the home. This removes them from a maternal and paternal setting and allows them to be themselves.

Recognize when an issue is about your in-laws and when it's really about you. One of the struggles I have had with my new family is quietly wondering if they really like me. All of my new family members have been kind, gracious, and giving at every turn, but from time to time I can't help but wonder: "Do these people really like me because of who I am or because they have to like me?" In other words, would these be people I would naturally hang out with given the choice, and would they naturally hang out with me? It's tough to know if your in-laws really like you. By the way, this confession reveals more about me and my insecurities than anything about them.

Look for ways to bless your in-laws. You may not get along with either your mother-in-law or father-in-law, but you can still bake cookies, drop by fresh flowers, and give other small gifts. In addition, you can write them a letter about the wonderful son or daughter they've raised. Brag to them about your spouse. Whether you want to admit it or not, they had a lot to do with the way your spouse turned out.

Not only do you have to get along with your in-laws, but also you have to get along with them for a very long time. Just a little extra pressure for you, as if you didn't already have enough.

Questions for Reflection

1. How would you describe your relationship with your in-laws? What steps could you take to strengthen the relationship?

2. How would you describe your spouse's relationship with your parents? What steps can you take to strengthen their relationship?

3. How can you incorporate your in-laws into your prayer list?

4. What one action could you do this week to bless your in-laws?

Conflict Resolution

One of the biggest differences many young couples discover is the way they handle conflict. You may want to deal with an issue now, but your partner may need time to process. One spouse may want to suppress feelings and emotions while another wants an immediate discussion.

One fellow who was brought up in a family of brothers said that he was brought up to settle things by wrestling. "Well, you can't do that with your wife," he says. "So I had to learn to handle things differently."

The key is identifying how you naturally respond to conflict and figure out which way works best for you as a couple. Unfortunately, a universal formula doesn't exist.

As a newlywed, Shana discovered that when an issue came up between her and her husband, it usually took a while to come to an understanding or solution. "We easily get defensive and exaggerate an issue," she says. "We're still learning how to deal with this. Last week we got in a little argument over something really stupid, and afterward I was pushing him to talk about how we can keep this from happening again. He reminded me that we're imperfect people, and we can't follow a formula and expect never to have a conflict again."

Some people need space during a conflict. Your spouse may require 10 or 15 minutes to cool off. Ask if there is anything you can do, and if the answer is no, then give your spouse the time he or she needs.

... continued

It is also important to notice if the same conflict emerges in different arguments. You may find a struggle for control, basic insecurity, or an issue of jealousy recurring in your arguments. Think about recent disagreements. Is there a common theme or pattern? Is there a common emotional response you have? What do these common traits reveal about you, your spouse, your pasts, or any unresolved issues in your relationship? Talk to your spouse about your frustrations and their source. If it is something from childhood, share the story so your spouse can have compassion.

Sometimes, though, your conflicts have nothing to do with your past or a sin in your life; rather, it's just a good, old-fashioned moment of selfishness. Filipe, a 23-year-old who has been married one year, says, "I feel like conflicts will happen every now and then simply because we are not always in tune with God's heart. What I have noticed is that the days that we are closest to God are the days we argue less. When we are spending time with Him and letting His Word work in us, we are so much more loving, more forgiving, more gentle, slower to speak, and quicker to listen."

nineteen | **Bumps in the Road**

All great marriages go through fighting, stagnation, and distance, and come out on the other side richer and more fulfilling.

—Carrie and Gary
Oliver

Rick Warren, author of the bestselling *Purpose-Driven Life*, says that after three decades in ministry, he noticed that it's not unusual for young couples to float through their first few years of marriage in love-blinded bliss. But the first two years of Rick and Kay Warren's marriage were the most difficult.

"If we both hadn't been committed to Jesus Christ and we both hadn't agreed that divorce was not an option, we wouldn't have stayed together," Warren says. "It was simply too difficult."

The young couple struggled in five of the main areas of marriage: money, sex, in-laws, children, and communication. "Because we knew we were in it for the long haul, we were forced to accept each other's differences. What else were we going to do?"

Warren says God helped the couple not only accept the differences but also appreciate them. The hard truth, according to Warren, is that marriage is a laboratory for developing God's love and attributes in you.*

SURPRISE NO. 30

While the wonders of marriage are really wonderful, the hardships of marriage are really hard.

This idea is supported by Gary Thomas in his book *Sacred Marriage,* in which he writes that marriage was not meant to make you happy; it was meant to make you holy. Marriage is one of the prime places where we are molded and shaped to become like Christ. The rough edges of our sinful nature are filed off over time as we are reshaped into the likeness of our Maker.

Unfortunately, there's no telling when the bumps in the road of marriage will surface. Sometimes they happen before the wedding day or after the honeymoon. Others find that difficulties don't surface until two, three, or five years later. But sooner or later they will emerge.

How do you handle the challenging points of marriage?

The first and most important way to combat marital difficulty is through prayer. The power of prayer in a marriage cannot be overstated. It has the ability to soften hearts, affect actions, and make a tremendous difference in a relationship.

It's also important to establish marital mentors and get counseling if needed. One of the biggest mistakes young couples often make is not seeking relationships with older married people who can help them. This can be done on a one-on-one or couple-to-couple basis. In addition, it's important to develop friendships with other young couples who are facing similar challenges. Depending

FOOTNOTE

*   Quotes taken from "The Purpose-Driven Marriage" by Rick Warren. *Marriage Partnership,* Summer 2004, pp. 27-30.

on the severity of the issue, a discussion with a close friend or an older couple in the church may provide insight or wisdom that will make the difference in your relationship. If the issue is more serious, you should consider seeking counsel from a trained marital professional or pastor. Could you talk to the person you married about getting marital counseling? Are there any counseling centers in your area? Do you know any other couples who have sought counseling who can refer you to an office?

Recognize that every relationship has different seasons. While romance novels would like you to believe that every moment is designed to be a tantalizing delight, the truth is that marriages naturally have ups and downs, moments of stagnation, and hurdles that must be overcome. During the first few months of marriage, your spouse may come home and greet you with passionate kisses and a "How did I live the day without you?" exchange. Eventually, this will tame into a passionate kiss, and then into a quick kiss, and then into a hug. If left unchecked, you may find yourself working in the living room unaware that your spouse came home at all. Being conscious that your heightened responses to each other will naturally lessen gives you the opportunity to be more intentional in expressing your affection as time goes on.

After the first or second year of marriage, the body chemistry that played a part in your initial attraction will naturally change. Be ready for it. Realize that it's normal.

Never entertain thoughts of divorce. Before divorce ever makes its way to a signed legal document, it begins in the heart and mind of a marriage partner. Resist the temptation to think of divorce as a way out or fantasize about how you would live if something suddenly happened to your spouse. This is dangerous ground with a slippery slope. There will be times when divorce may seem like the easy way out, but it never is and it was not part of God's original plan for marriage.

Quick Tip: Order a pizza and eat it by candlelight.

Recognize that the issue you're facing may not be about your spouse as much as it is about you. Madeline, a 37-year-old who has been married for six years, says that she is constantly wrestling with petty frustrations. Her husband has a tendency to throw things away. No matter what it is or who it belongs to, if it is in the way, it is fair game for the trash can.

"I'm a 'stuff' person; I always have piles of paper and stuff," she says. "I would never throw his things away. I couldn't figure out why he just wouldn't put my stuff on the bed or somewhere out of his way. Why did he have to toss it?"

One day when Madaline was particularly frustrated over this issue and digging items that were important to her out of the garbage can, she felt the Holy Spirit whisper in her heart, "You have a husband who cleans."

"And I was like, oh yeah, I do," she recalls. "How many women would love to have someone like that? He throws things away because he likes things clean. He also cooks, takes care of the kitchen, and does a lot more sweeping and mopping than I do."

Sometimes you have to take a step back from your relationship and look at what God has given you—the spouse He's entrusted you with—and realize that the things that might be frustrating to you are things other women wish their husbands would do.

Try to understand. Many of the ways your spouse interacts with you are based on his or her upbringing. If you dig around your spouse's childhood long enough, you'll find clues as to why your mate responds a particular way. Unfortunately, there are some aspects of your spouse that you'll never understand. Your spouse may not be able to put into words why he or she acts or reacts in a certain way, leaving you to compromise and extend grace.

Resist the urge to withdraw. When a situation becomes stressful or overwhelming, my first reaction is to shut down and retreat. I don't want to put myself in a position where I can get hurt. This response is a very dangerous pattern that can undermine a healthy relationship, and it's one I have to continually battle. If my husband and I are going to get through a situation, then we're going to have to be able to talk about it, and waiting doesn't usually help. To combat my retreating nature, my husband clearly asks me, "Please don't withdraw," at which point I realize my personal weakness in this area and pray for the courage to express what I'm really thinking and feeling. It's a tough hurdle to overcome, but it's essential for a strong relationship.

Avoid saying "I'm sorry." It may sound a little strange, but "I'm sorry" isn't the best way to admit that you were wrong because "I'm sorry" really isn't an apology. What are you sorry for? Are you sorry for the way you made me feel or the way you feel? Or are you just sorry this became an issue in the first place? When you're apologizing, say the words "I was wrong" and ask the person to forgive you. If possible, suggest ways that you can actually prevent the same situation from developing again. Remember that the way you deliver an apology has a tremendous impact on its effectiveness. If you're slouching or refuse to look the person in the eye, the apology can come off as insincere and meaningless. Instead, apologize when you really mean it and express it in a way that demonstrates you really are sorry.

Avoid bad-mouthing your spouse. You may be tempted to unleash the anger or hurt you have in your heart when you're talking to friends, but be wary of painting a bad picture—and one that can't be easily corrected—of your spouse. While it's wise to seek counsel, avoid seeking opportunities or conversations where you can justify your position or make yourself feel better by criticizing your spouse. It will cost you dearly later on.

Recognize that this, too, will pass. While an issue may seem insurmountable today, it probably won't be as big six months or a year down the road. The size and shape of whatever you're facing will eventually change, and you'll change along with it. Never give up hope—in your marriage or the fact that God is in your marriage.

Focus on the positive. You will always be able to find an area of your relationship or something about your spouse that needs improvement. Yet Scripture challenges us to focus on those things which are honorable and good. Everyone has faults. Focusing on them will only make them bigger. Instead, make a mental list of things you love and appreciate about your spouse and the marriage you are building together.

During your first few years of marriage, you have the ability to lay a strong and powerful foundation. Whether you realize it or not, you're establishing habits and patterns for resolving conflict and handling difficulties. You're developing reactions and responses as a couple, and it's important to establish healthy ones.

Questions for Reflection

1. Where do you turn when you hit a bump in the road in your marriage?

2. How can you make bumps in the road opportunities for drawing closer to God?

3. What steps can you take to develop relationships with godly mentors as well as young couples?

4. How do conflicts and difficulties give you the opportunity to grow both individually and spiritually?

Twenty-Five Ways to Say I Love You

one Order a custom-made cake with "I love you" written on it.

two Call in a dedication on your partner's favorite radio station.

three Have flowers delivered in person by a mutual friend.

four Post a dedication on Lovingyou.com.

five Commission a billboard on your partner's route to work.

six Diamonds. Enough said.

seven Send a framed photograph of yourself, autographed by you.

eight Leave a loving message on voicemail or cell phone.

nine Leave little love notes around the house where your mate will find them.

ten Write something mushy on the bathroom mirror.

eleven Mail a letter, postcard, or greeting card.

twelve Commission a skywriter to write "I love you" in the air.

thirteen Announce your love for your spouse over the public address system in any public place.

... continued

fourteen Write a love poem.

fifteen Build a website dedicated to your love.

sixteen Take out an ad in the newspaper or a favorite magazine.

seventeen Make a screen saver and have a colleague load it onto your spouse's work computer.

eighteen Create a simple craft and send it to your love with a note.

nineteen Send a box of chocolates with a card.

twenty Write a love letter.

twenty-one Have an artist draw their portrait from a photograph.

twenty-two Carve a heart into a favorite tree.

twenty-three Buy something your mate has always wanted.

twenty-four Commission a love song sung just for your spouse.

twenty-five Commission a romance novel with the both of you as the lead characters.*

FOOTNOTE

* Adapted From: 25 Ways to Say I Love You by Bob Narindra, www.lovingyou.com/content/married/content.shtml?ART=25waystosay. Used with permission.

The Wonders of Married Life

twenty

Those who follow Christ have a much better chance at accomplishing the Bible's odd mathematics of marriage, of making two become one. Why? Because such people bring an expectation of gradual growth to their marriage. They expect time to act as their friend as they live together.

—DAVID MAINS

ANYONE WHO HAS WORN A WEDDING RING for very long will tell you—marriage isn't easy. And then they'll tag on that little phrase you learn to love to hate, "Marriage is a lot of work." When I first heard this statement, I thought it was an honest and wise reflection on the mysterious nature of two people becoming one. But years later, after I've heard the same phrase echoed more than a hundred times, it's lost some of its luster. Now that I'm married, I'm beginning to wonder what that statement really means.

Marriage is work, but what does that "work" look like? Does it mean doing countless loads of laundry, vacuuming miles of carpet, and emptying the dishwasher load after load? Does it mean packing and unloading boxes every time we move? Does it mean carrying a child for nine months and experiencing what looks to be some horrific painful poking and prodding to produce a baby that will share our last name (or names)? Does it mean being patient when my spouse snaps at me or showing kindness when I'm spent? Does it mean reaching out and praying for the one I love when my only real prayers are for myself?

I think it means all of those things and more.

SURPRISE NO. 31

Marriage takes lots of work, and all that work takes a lot of different forms.

The "work" that is required in a marriage involves many different forms of self-sacrifice, so that when someone says "marriage is work," they are using it as an umbrella or catchall phrase to remind us (and themselves) that marriage isn't all about receiving. In fact, it's just the opposite.

When two people come together in marriage—especially with a mutual commitment that says divorce is not an option—the wonders of marriage begin to unfold. Being with your best friend. Never having to say goodbye. Always having someone there.

Leif and I have discovered a few of those wonders. We enjoy taking long walks together, reading books side-by-side, and watching movies on our laptop, which requires us to sit shoulder to shoulder. We have designated do-nothing days which are filled with lounging on the couch, renting DVDs, eating junk food, and you-know-what. Sometimes, late at night, we'll go to McDonald's and order dipped ice cream cones (which we've nicknamed "conos" after the Spanish

Quick Tip: Turn the radio to the station your spouse enjoys.

pronunciation), sit, and talk. We love our cono treats, but we love more the time together. We are thrilled whenever we have the opportunity to travel with each other and snuggle in our passenger seats for an entire flight. We love to lie on the floor of our living room and recount the day's events. We love being together and being connected emotionally, physically, and spiritually.

But the wonders of marriage extend beyond what we do together into the things I see in him that I don't think he sees in himself. Several weeks ago we were walking down the road together and he noticed that someone's trash can had blown into the stream. He risked his dry tennis shoes and wet feet to be the unsung hero who retrieved the trash can. I was the only human who witnessed his kind act. Even though he wasn't doing it for me, it still touched my heart. Or the privilege of watching him lie on the couch, read his Bible, and take time to reflect and pray. Or the moments I get to see him do quiet acts of service and kindness for unknowing friends and neighbors. These are just a few of the moments that make me stand in wonder.

> Finally, brothers, whatever is true, whatever is noble, whatever is right, whatever is pure, whatever is lovely, whatever is admirable—if anything is excellent or praiseworthy—think about such things.
>
> —PHILIPPIANS 4:8

I bet you have a few stories like these about your own spouse.

Ralph, a 34-year-old who has been married since he was 19, describes what he loves most about married life: "I love being known by my wife. I like having a mocha at Starbucks and having someone to share it with. I like getting that spot scratched in the middle of my back that I could never get to by myself. I love it when I'm in a room full of people and we catch each other's eyes and give each other that 'Hey, Baby, want to get lucky' look and then get to go home and do something about it without the guilt.

"I love waking up with her head curled up to my chest. I love going home knowing that she is there, even if she is mad at me for playing golf. I love being loved. I love pooling together all of our loose change and going to buy ice cream and sharing it. I love the smell of her perfume on my workout clothes."

Rodney has tapped into some of the wonders of marriage. Hopeless romantic? Maybe. But isn't there something that God placed within the human heart that longs for romance?

SURPRISE NO. 32

The wonders of marriage are more wonderful than I ever could have imagined.

Or take Mara, a 24-year-old who has been married for a little more than a year. She believes it's the little things—whether having coffee in the morning, traveling together, or eating at their favorite restaurant—that make marriage wonderful. "I love living together," she says. "When we were dating, we had to be so careful not to be alone and not to give a bad appearance. Now there's freedom! I love how every night we pray together before we fall asleep, and I love watching movies at home. The best thing is knowing that there's something or someone there for me no matter what."

Like a fingerprint, no other couple on the planet is quite like you and your spouse. No one has the exact same mix of values, beliefs, strengths, weaknesses, and interests, and thus you are given the opportunity to grow, develop, and strengthen your relationship in amazing ways.

Marriage makes people stronger. Studies have shown that married people, particularly men, tend to live longer than people who aren't married. Both married men and women have more assets than singles on average, and they are also able to combine their knowledge on everything from home repair to cooking to financial planning.

Quick Tip: Plan something special for your anniversary.

The wonders of marriage are wrapped up in the possibilities of having a partner—someone you can face the challenges of this life with. Someone you can stay up late with thinking, dreaming, and planning a future together. Someone you can express every feeling to and know you can count on. Someone you can share your life and your innermost being with—those are just a few of the wonders of marriage. And while it might take some work and a sharp eye to recognize some of the hidden wonders, they're well worth the effort.

Questions for Reflection

1. What are some of the wonders of your marriage? What little things do you do with your spouse that make you smile inside? What makes your spouse smile inside?

2. What are some of the activities you most enjoy doing with your spouse? What can you do to make sure you take time to do those activities?

3. What is the foundation your marriage is based upon? Do you have "divorce is not an option" as part of your commitment?

The Perks

Anniversary Gift List

Seven Things to Do with the Wedding Gifts You Never Wanted

Communication 101: Tough Questions That Are Rarely Asked

It's Never Too Early to Establish Traditions

Handling PDB (Public Displays of Bickering)

Five Tips for Having a Great Date

Anniversary Gift List

Year	Traditional	Modern	Alternative/Modern
1	paper	plastics	clocks
2	cotton	cotton/calico	china
3	leather	leather	crystal/glass
4	fruit/flowers	linen/silk/nylon	appliances
5	wood	wood	silverware
6	candy/iron	iron	wood
7	copper/wool	copper/wool/brass	desk sets
8	bronze/pottery	bronze/appliances	linens
9	pottery/willow	pottery	leather
10	tin	aluminum	diamond
11	steel	steel	jewelry
12	silk/linen	silk/linen	pearl
13	lace	lace	textiles/fur
14	ivory	ivory	gold
15	crystal	glass	watches
20	china	china	platinum
25	silver	silver	silver
30	pearl	pearl	pearl
35	coral	coral/jade	jade
40	ruby	ruby/garnet	ruby
45	sapphire	sapphire	sapphire
50	gold	gold	gold
55	emerald	emerald/turquoise	emerald
60	diamond	gold	diamond
75	diamond	diamond/gold	diamond

(Taken from: www.compendia.info/anniversary_gifts.htm)

Seven Things to Do with the Wedding Gifts You Never Wanted

one *Return the gift.* This is the top choice for most couples, especially when you receive duplicates. Either a refund or an exchange will suffice. But sometimes you just can't figure out where the purple-and-blue floral towels with golden ruffles were purchased. (That's why there are six other ideas on the list.)

two *Spread the love.* Remember that some wedding gifts are like fruit-cake; they just keep passing from person to person year after year. At least one or two of the wedding gifts you received were from someone else's wedding. I'm sorry if no one told you this before, but there were probably a few couples at your wedding who didn't like their gifts and have been holding onto them and waiting for the perfect moment to place them back into the eternal recycle bin of wedding gifts. Please don't take it personally. It's not that they don't like you; it's just that they didn't know who else might like it. And you were the best choice. If you don't care for this particular gift, you can always return the favor.

One woman I spoke with received a silver tray for her wedding. When she read the card and ripped off the wrapping paper, she discovered another wedding card inside. It was written to the couple who gave her the tray! The couple had received the gift at their own wedding but never bothered to open the box. Busted! So the woman waited until the next wedding she attended and slipped her wedding card, along with the original card, in the box and passed along the gift. She never heard a peep from the couple who received the double recycled gift. To this day, it's a mystery. But if you happen to receive a silver tray with a stack of wedding cards inside, please let us know.

... continued

three *Keep this gift as a discussion piece.* One of my closest friends gave us our most memorable wedding gift: a hollow wooden frog. It has a dowel in its mouth, and when you pull it out and rub the frog's grooved back, it makes a "ribbit" sound. It's not your typical wedding gift. When I first saw it, I thought, "Why?" But it quickly became one of my favorite gifts because it was so quirky and thoughtful and represented the person who gave it to me. Whenever the discussion dies down during an evening with friends, we can pull out our trusty wooden frog.

four *Sell the gift at a garage sale.* You may think that's a ridiculous idea now, but just wait six or eight months. You'll be putting a little yellow sticker with a hand-written price tag on it and praying someone buys it. Just make sure the person who gave it to you doesn't live in the area and like to go to garage sales on Saturday morning.

five *Donate the gift to charity.* How about a tax write-off from Uncle Sam for your unneeded wedding gift? This may be scraping the bottom of the barrel of options, but what else do you think you can do with the framed print of a hand-drawn aardvark?

six *Throw the gift away.* This one can be a toughy, especially if you're close to the people who gave you the gift. But depending on how ugly or useless the gift is—and yes, there are some real doozies out there—it may deserve the trash can, even though this will mean breaking the recycling of the never-ending wedding gifts.

seven *Store it forever.* This should be your last resort option. But sometimes—call it sentimental—you just can't get rid of it. And that's fine. Just plan on doing a year's worth of dusting and cleaning to maintain your treasure.

Communication 101: Tough Questions That Are Rarely Asked

Believe it or not, there are some issues many couples never talk about their whole lives. If you haven't discussed any of these questions in depth, you may want to find a time to discuss the following:

one What are a few of your happiest memories of family experiences?

two What is one of your unhappiest family memories? How did you and your family deal with this unpleasant experience?

three What did your parents do that assured you of their love for you?

four What do you wish your parents would have said or done to show you their love?

five Have you ever been abused?

six What were your parents' best attributes?

seven What addictions did people in your family experience? What unmet needs might have contributed to those addictions?

eight What do you most often worry about?

nine Are you sometimes surprised by your own sudden feelings of anger? How do you respond when other people drive poorly, are late or forget meetings, make messes, or act selfishly?*

FOOTNOTE

*   Thanks to Gene Skinner for his insightful help on developing these.

It's Never Too Early to Establish Traditions

WHENEVER MY HUSBAND AND I TRAVEL and rent a car, we name the car. I know that sounds kind of strange and maybe even a little silly, but every car has an official naming ceremony as we drive it off the lot. We've driven Beth, Shorty, Sam, Allie, Joe, Pokey, and Stinky (the previous renter had decided to light up a cigarette), among others. As you can tell, we rent a lot of economy cars, believing money is better spent on the hotel and meals. As a couple we've decided to invest in being there rather than getting there, and we have driven in some extremely compact cars as a result. But every so often we get upgraded and enjoy driving Alexander, Roberto, or Maxamillion, whom we called Max for short.

On a recent trip to Miami, my husband and I got upgraded to a luxury minivan—and no, those words are not an oxymoron—complete with leather seats and enough gadgets and gizmos to qualify us for an old episode of *Miami Vice*. Feeling like Trump, we named the car Donald and enjoyed cruising between Miami and Palm Beach.

Naming our rental cars has become more than a tradition for us. It's become a great way to break up the monotony of travel and add humor to the sometimes stressful moments of getting lost in a new city. When we wonder where our car is in the parking lot, we simply call him or her by name. Though the car never answers back—I promise—we have a lot of fun.

Traditions add a richness to life. They serve as markers to the past and reminders of the faithfulness of God in a relationship. Traditions bring back rich memories and create a heritage for future generations. They can impart wisdom, reverence, hope, and laughter. They also anchor you in a relationship and create a sense of consistency so that no matter where you live or what age and stage of life you're in, there's a still familiar rhythm to life that lets you know things are going to be all right.

It's no wonder that God was such a big fan of feasts, celebrations, holidays, and the rich traditions they contain. Passover, for example, was a unique holiday in the sense that it was created to commemorate an event that hadn't occurred yet. Think about that for a moment. Most of our holidays wouldn't exist unless something significant took place. We wouldn't have Fourth of July without our nation's independence or Veteran's Day without war. There wouldn't be Thanksgiving without the Pilgrims or Christmas without Christ. But God told the people of Israel to celebrate Passover before they were delivered from slavery in Egypt.

> The LORD said to Moses and Aaron in Egypt, "This month is to be for you the first month, the first month of your year. Tell the whole community of Israel that on the tenth day of this month each man is to take a lamb for his family, one for each household. If any household is too small for a whole lamb, they must share one with their nearest neighbor, having taken into account the number of people there are. You are to

determine the amount of lamb needed in accordance
with what each person will eat. The animals you
choose must be year-old males without defect, and you
may take them from the sheep or the goats. Take care
of them until the fourteenth day of the month, when
all the people of the community of Israel must
slaughter them at twilight. Then they are to take some
of the blood and put it on the sides and tops of the
doorframes of the houses where they eat the lambs.
That same night they are to eat the meat roasted over
the fire, along with bitter herbs, and bread made
without yeast. Do not eat the meat raw or cooked in
water, but roast it over the fire—head, legs and inner
parts. Do not leave any of it till morning; if some is
left till morning, you must burn it. This is how you
are to eat it: with your cloak tucked into your belt,
your sandals on your feet and your staff in your hand.
Eat it in haste; it is the Lord's Passover" (Exodus 12:1-
11 NIV).

God was extremely specific about His instructions for the
Passover. If you'll take the time to read the rest of the chapter, you'll
discover that He commanded the people to observe the Passover
for generations to come. He specifically commands:

Obey these instructions as a lasting ordinance for
you and your descendants. When you enter the land
that the Lord will give you as he promised, observe
this ceremony. And when your children ask you, "What
does this ceremony mean to you?" then tell them, "It
is the Passover sacrifice to the Lord, who passed over
the houses of the Israelites in Egypt and spared our
homes when he struck down the Egyptians." Then the
people bowed down and worshiped (Exodus 12:24-27).

Four Things to Keep in Mind for Establishing Traditions

1. *Choose traditions that work for you.* There are as many traditions as there are couples. Find which traditions work for you and your spouse. Talk about them. If your spouse isn't fond of the idea, work together to develop a tradition that you both can agree upon and enjoy.

2. *Pull traditions from your heritage.* Which traditions does your family keep? Which holidays have special meanings, rituals, or celebrations attached to them? Discuss family traditions from both sides and decide which ones you want to bring into your marriage and future family.

3. *Think long-term about your traditions.* For example, if you're living in Alaska, you may choose to build a snowman every Christmas. But if you move to Florida, you may have to come up with a new tradition or learn to build a snowman out of sand on the beach.

4. *Be creative with your traditions.* Remember that you don't have to have a holiday to have a tradition. While some traditions should carry spiritual depth and meaning, others can just be fun. Bake crazy cakes. Eat breakfast for dinner. Hike a particular trail. Get away to your favorite bed-and-breakfast. Watch Nascar or a bowl game together. Watch movies all day and eat pizza. Enjoy being together and celebrating the life God's given you.

God had many reasons for commanding celebration, one of the most significant being the foreshadowing of the coming Messiah. But it's interesting to note that one of God's reasons for His command to observe the Passover was so the children would become curious about the tradition. Eventually, they would be tempted to ask their parents about the tradition. Mom and dad would be given an opportunity to share their faith with the next generation.

So when you're thinking about traditions you want to form with your spouse, consider some that have spiritual implications. For example, my husband and I have begun praying over every home we move into. We thank God for His provision. One day I hope our children will be able to partake in that same tradition. As for other traditions, we're still in the process of establishing them. Many holiday traditions—including Easter, Thanksgiving, Christmas, and New Year's—are still under construction. We're in the planning stages of discovering what works for us.

If you're still determining what works for you, that's okay too. Just make sure that you're intentional about establishing traditions. Don't let too many years slip by without trying something new—even if it's naming your rental cars. Oh, and for those of you who are still wondering how we determine the gender of the car we're renting, that's easy. We just look under the hood.

Handling PDB (Public Displays of Bickering)

Almost everyone gives newlyweds a little extra grace for PDA—Public Displays of Affection. A little more hand holding. Sitting a little closer. A longer-than-usual smooch. All of those quiet pats, quickie back rubs, butt pinches, and tender touches are not only excused but quietly smiled upon when you're a newlywed.

But there's a different type of public display that often occurs when you're newly married that isn't quite as endearing. It's something I like to call PDB—Public Displays of Bickering—and it strikes most newlyweds within the first few months (if not weeks) of marriage.

By now you're probably thinking that this section is for *other* newlyweds. PDB doesn't apply to *us*, we're too much in love. I used to think the same thing. But then when I watched the way we interact when we were together with others, I realized that Leif and I were just as guilty as any other couple. No, we didn't technically argue with each other in front of others or raise our voices, but we still bickered in our own way—subtly wrestling with details, accuracy, and the way each of us remembered a story—which, it turns out, is usually very different!

PDB takes many forms. Correcting each other's sentences. Adding details when the person is fully capable of telling the story. Finishing a story because the spouse telling it is taking too long. Interjecting ideas, thoughts, and inside jokes.

Our bickering usually stems from differences in our personalities. Leif is a master storyteller. He has hundreds of great stories from his childhood—like the time he threw water balloons at a fire truck on its way back from an emergency and ran into the woods to hide. A few hours later, a policeman knocked on his door. Leif had left the bucket full of the remaining water balloons by the side of the road. Unfortunately, his name and address were written in permanent marker on the side of the bucket.

Leif has enough of these tales to create his own book or video series, and he has a way of captivating listeners as he spins his tales. The only problem is that sometimes the numbers or descriptions may get a little exaggerated for effect.

As a journalist, this tendency drives me nuts. I'm concerned with accuracy, consistency, things that matter in great news reporting—and think that truly great storytelling is only great if it's true. At times I can't help but slip in a quiet reminder, "Are you sure it was that many?" or shoot him the look that says, "Give me a break." And those moments usually come at the climax of the story—so I have to hold my tongue. But sometimes I can't help myself; I interject and fall into the trap of the PDB.

In our PDB, neither of us is really right. If left unchecked, I become a control freak and accuracy checker, and he becomes an

> **Quick Ways to Avoid PDB**
> - Give your spouse the grace to be wrong.
> - Remember that you're not right all the time either.
> - Refuse to correct your spouse in public. Do it in private.
> - Remember that people naturally remember stories differently.

exaggerator—neither of which are Christlike or very becoming qualities. But I am slowly learning to let things go in public and talk
to him behind closed doors about the stories that got out of hand.
In the end, we make it a smoother ride not only for ourselves, but
also for everyone we're with too.

Five Tips for Having a Great Date

Quick Quiz: When was the last time you and your husband headed out for a really great date?

a) *Last night.*

b) *In the last seven nights.*

c) *In the last two weeks.*

d) *In the last month.*

e) *I can't quite remember.*

IF YOU ANSWERED (A) OR (B), YOU'RE IN THE MINORITY. If you answered (c), (d), or even (e), you're among the masses. Despite the quiet promises we all make to ourselves, most partners in a marriage find themselves consumed with meeting the daily demands of life. At the end of the day, time, energy, or money for a romantic getaway may seem nonexistent.

But you can make a change. David and Claudia Arp, authors of *10 Great Dates to Energize Your Marriage* and *52 Dates for You and*

Your Mate (available at www.marriagealive.com), offer some tips to get you started.

1. *Take the initiative.* Don't wait for him to ask you out. Study your schedules and find a night that will work for both of you. Hire a sitter or ask a neighbor or friend to take the kids for an evening. Plan on eating together—whether it's a romantic dinner in or a nice evening out—and some sort of activity afterward. Go to the movies. Attend a concert. Take a walk. Make a dessert together. The bottom line is: Be intentional about spending time together.

2. *Plan a date around something your husband loves to do.* If he likes basketball, surprise him with two tickets to a local game. If he loves video games, take him (and a bag of quarters) to an arcade. If he loves collectibles, take him to an antique show. Make the date center around something he loves—even if it's not your favorite thing to do—and enjoy making his face light up.

3. *Plan a variety of dates.* The Arps' *52 Dates for You and Your Mate* gives dating suggestions by categories, such as romantic dates, cheap and easy dates, getting in shape dates, and even we're-just-too-tired dates. Variety is the spice of life and will certainly spice up your marriage. When the Arps are exhausted, the couple has a "We're Just Too Tired to Talk Date." Together, they agree to ignore the phone, order takeout for dinner, put in a video, and snuggle on the couch.

4. *Be creative.* Try a formal dinner in the park. Dress up, pack a tablecloth, candles, and classical music, and pick up food on the way. Try a blue highway date. Don't take any four-lane roads or stop at chain restaurants. See what you can discover in a 50-mile radius of your home. Have a window-shopping date but with a different twist. Look and pick out all the things you already have. You can turn this into a "grateful" date!

5. *Remember the importance of dates.* For married couples, dating helps you to be intentional and to focus on each other. Dating helps

to build your friendship and keeps your relationship alive and growing. Don't talk about work, kids, or your in-laws. Focus just on you. If you want to energize your marriage, keep your dates about just the two of you.*

* Portions of this section originally appeared in an article I wrote for Renewingtheheart.com.

About the Author

Margaret Feinberg is still a newlywed. On September 20, 2003, she said "I do" to a 6'8" Norwegian who stole her heart. Margaret and her husband, Leif, currently reside in Sitka, Alaska. They enjoy traveling, hanging out with friends, and looking for the Northern Lights on cold winter nights together.

You can contact the author at

margaret@margaretfeinberg.com,
www.margaretfeinberg.com,

or in care of Harvest House Publishers
990 Owen Loop North, Eugene, OR 97402.

Other Good Harvest House Reading

The Power of a Praying® Wife
Stormie Omartian

Bestselling author Stormie Omartian shares how wives can develop a deeper relationship with their husbands by praying for them. Packed with practical advice on praying for specific areas, including: decision making, fears, spiritual strength, and sexuality, women will discover the fulfilling marriage God intended.

The Power of a Praying® Husband
Stormie Omartian

This effective guide encourages men to prayerfully intercede for their wives in areas including motherhood, priorities, emotions, and sexuality. Chapters feature comments from well-known Christian men, biblical wisdom, and prayer ideas.

Becoming the Woman of His Dreams
Sharon Jaynes

Becoming the Woman of His Dreams is a thoughtful look at the wonderful, unique, and God-ordained role a woman has in her husband's life. Sharon Jaynes offers seven key qualities every wife should strive for.

Men Are Like Waffles—Women Are Like Spaghetti
Bill and Pam Farrel

Men keep life elements in separate boxes; women intertwine everything. Providing biblical insights, sound research, and humorous anecdotes, the Farrels explore gender differences and preferences and how they can strengthen relationships.